A YEAR OF POSITIVE THINKING FOR TEENS

A YEAR OF POSITIVE THINKING FOR TEENS

DAILY MOTIVATION TO BEAT STRESS, INSPIRE HAPPINESS, AND ACHIEVE YOUR GOALS

KATIE HURLEY, LCSW

ROCKRIDGE
PRESS

Interior and Cover Designer: Brian Lewis
Art Producer: Karen Williams
Editors: Meera Pal and Samantha Holland
Production Editor: Emily Sheehan
All images used under license © BosotochkaArt/Creative Market.
Author photo courtesy of Daniel Doty Photography.

ISBN: Print 978-1-64739-640-4 | eBook 978-1-64739-387-8
R2

For Riley and Liam

CONTENTS

INTRODUCTION

Looking back, I'm fairly certain I spent most of my teen years in a state of functional stress. Don't get me wrong! I had a lot of fun in middle school and high school, but I also put a ton of pressure on myself to measure up to some set of perceived standards that I created. I worried about my grades every day. I worried about my performance on my soccer, hockey, and lacrosse teams and where I was on each of the lineups. I worried about social issues. Though I had a lot of friends, I didn't fit into one specific group, and I felt left out at times. I worried about getting into college and what my future would hold. School came with a lot of worry and stress. The problem, however, was that I didn't know how to deal with that stress.

Movies and television shows have a way of making the teen years look like a giant pep rally, but being a teen can be hard. You have your own stressors to deal with on any given day. Homework, friendships, family expectations, and navigating the day-to-day activities of life are incredibly stressful. If you feel like you're overloaded by stress right now, please know that you are not alone. But knowing that you are not alone isn't always enough. Wouldn't it be even better to know how to reduce or to manage the stress you're feeling?

Several years after high school, in a psychology class at Boston College, something we were studying resulted in a moment of clarity that has since stuck with me: Our thought processes play a vital role in how we experience our day-to-day lives. Positive thinking creates feelings of hopefulness and empowers us to take the necessary steps to promote positive outcomes, while negative thinking can cloud our ability to work through difficult experiences and result in feelings of hopelessness. While there are a lot of things we simply cannot control in life, one thing we can control is how we respond to people, experiences, and stress.

Realistically, no one feels happy and positive every minute of every day. To be human is to endure life's ups and downs, make mistakes, and experience uncomfortable emotions, especially during the important teen years. Between academics, friends, social media, extracurriculars, and everything else on any given day, there are plenty of opportunities for hardship and stress. But here is the good news: You can work through the stress and negativity to bring positivity back into your life, and learning to engage in positive thinking is a crucial first step.

You may be wondering how positive thinking can help you get through the hard stuff; it sounds too simple, right? After two decades of working with teens, I've had several conversations that ended with some version of "whatever you say, Katie" followed by joint laughter. (Yes, therapists *do* actually laugh and have fun with their clients.) Here's the thing: Research actually shows that positive thoughts and imagery can help you work through negative feelings. Researchers from King's College in London tested this theory with people who have anxiety, asking them to visualize positive outcomes or imagery when thinking about their worries. After people in the study completed the visualization exercise, they reported lower anxiety and increased happiness.

Barbara Fredrickson, professor of psychology and neuroscience at the University of North Carolina at Chapel Hill, wrote a book called *Positivity* that helps people harness the power of positive thinking to work through stress. In one of her studies, Fredrickson found that positive thinking actually broadens the feeling of possibility. Fredrickson calls this the "broaden and build" theory. Positive emotions actually broaden your mind and allow you to build new skills and resources.

However, positive thinking isn't as easy as coming up with a happy memory in your brain every time you feel stressed. In fact, Fredrickson advises that it takes about three positive thoughts to outweigh one negative thought. As it turns out, negative thoughts are heavy. I'm sure you've experienced the heaviness of negative feelings at some point, like those days when you feel like you just want to hide in your room.

I've learned from working with teens that every teen is different; everyone has their own unique feelings and experiences. While it helps to know the positive-to-negative thought ratio, it's also important to focus on your own thought processes. I often tell my teen clients that the first step is to get to know our negative thinking. What kinds of thoughts tend to flood your brain when you're stressed, bored, or lonely? Negative thoughts often follow a pattern. When we listen to them and get to know them, we learn how to work through and silence them.

As I sat in that psychology classroom all those years ago, I realized that my negative thoughts boiled down to two things: *This is too hard for you,* and *You'll never measure up.* Once I recognized these patterns, I learned to develop positive thoughts to counter them and found a strategy that worked for me: Say the negative thought out loud, own it, and "talk back" to it using the positive thoughts (or mantras) I practiced each day.

There's one other thing you need to know about positive thinking: It takes practice. Practice, practice, practice. My teen clients often tell me they worry positive thinking just isn't working because it only seems to work some of the time. Learning to change your thinking won't happen overnight. You should expect some ups and downs as you get to know your own thought processes and find what works for you. That's perfectly okay. If you stick with it, you'll find that it does come naturally with time.

My greatest hope for you is that the wisdom, strategies, and inspirational quotes in this book help guide you toward a new way of coping with hardship and stress. By reading just one entry every day, you're benefitting from positive thinking and positive psychology. Soon, you'll build resilience, learn to work through negative emotions, and develop your own unique coping kit. Being a teen isn't easy. I hope this book helps you find the courage you need to overcome adversity and achieve your goals. Most of all, I hope it gives you the strength to keep going when the world feels overwhelming.

Are you ready to view the world through a different lens and make time for positive change? Let's take this journey together.

JANUARY

1

Be Present

You are exactly where you're supposed to be. You don't have to set big goals just because it's a new year; you simply need to accept where you are and start there.

Maybe you don't like where you are right now. Maybe you're struggling with something, wishing you had more friends, or feeling overwhelmed with school. That's okay. Be present in the difficult moments, and you will be able to find your way out.

If you're feeling like you're in a good place, slow down and embrace it. Pay attention to what is going well and why. This will help you remember what you need to do to feel positive when things are hard.

Start the first day of the new year right by embracing the present:

I am where I am supposed to be.
I am always learning and growing.
I am on my own path.

2
JANUARY

Step Outside Your Comfort Zone

"You cannot swim for new horizons until
you have courage to lose sight of the shore."

—WILLIAM FAULKNER, *THE MANSION*

Sometimes we avoid new experiences because we're afraid that we might fail or get lost along the way. But overcoming obstacles and finding your own path can be fun and exciting.

Step outside your comfort zone. At the beginning of each month, write down three new things you want to try or have always wanted to experience. Commit to trying one of the new things on your list this month. Remember to take small steps and give yourself the time and compassion to learn.

3
JANUARY

Believe in Yourself

Your thoughts affect your actions. When you tell yourself you can do something, believe that you can do it. When you believe in your own abilities, you set yourself up to keep going. Cheer yourself on every single day by finishing these sentences:

Something I am good at is . . .
My friends like to be around me because . . .
I help others by . . .

4
JANUARY

Own Your Strengths

We all have strengths and weaknesses in various areas of our lives. If you focus on your weaknesses, you are only looking for problems. But if you focus on your strengths, you will discover solutions.

You have what it takes to make your own dreams come true. Overcome any obstacle by owning your strengths and enjoy little successes along the way.

5

See the Beauty in Change

*"We delight in the beauty of the butterfly,
but rarely admit the changes it has gone
through to achieve that beauty."*

—MAYA ANGELOU

6
JANUARY

Plant Your Dreams

Dreams are like seeds. You can plant them, nurture them, and bring them to life. Your thoughtful actions and your imagination are the water and sun that help your dreams grow and bloom. It takes time and daily practice to grow your seeds, but each little step brings your dreams closer to reality.

7

Your Potential is Unlimited

Create the life that you want and reach your goals: believe in yourself, be open to new ideas and opportunities, take chances, and accept failure.

When you believe in your own potential, you open new doors and give yourself the chance to grow.

8
JANUARY

One Day at a Time

"Don't worry about a week or a month from now—just think about one day at a time. If you are worried about the mountain in the distance, you might trip over the molehill right in front of you. Win the day!"

**—DREW BREES, COMING BACK STRONGER:
UNLEASHING THE HIDDEN POWER OF ADVERSITY**

Check In With Your Senses

Some days will feel overwhelming, and that's okay. It's hard to feel positive every second of every day. It's important to accept each day as it comes, but you can also work through your negative feelings. Take time for a mindful moment to shift your thinking. Ground yourself and take three deep breaths.

- What are three things you can see?
- What are three things you can hear?
- What are three things you can smell?
- What are three things you can feel?

10

Aim High

"The moment you doubt whether you can fly,
you cease forever to be able to do it."

—J. M. BARRIE, *THE LITTLE WHITE BIRD*

11

Your Thoughts Can Change

We all have negative thoughts from time to time. But *you* have the power to reframe your thoughts. You can take a worrisome thought and change it into a confident one just by using your words.

Try replacing your *what if* thoughts with *I can* or *I will*, which are more positive and uplifting. When you shift your thinking, your negative thoughts become smaller and harder to hear.

12

~

Setbacks Don't Define You

Everyone experiences setbacks. Part of reaching for your dreams is about taking chances. Some of those chances will push you toward your end goal, but some will set you back. What matters is not that you experience setbacks but that you take a moment to evaluate and learn from them. Setbacks are like little bumps in the road, but if you slow down and get to know where they come from, you can learn to navigate around them.

The next time you encounter a setback, close your eyes and think about what you can learn and take away from the experience. Ask yourself:

What was I trying to achieve?
What got in the way?
What can I do differently when I try again?

Your setbacks don't define you. How you rise up to meet challenges and overcome obstacles shows the world what you're made of.

Be Playful

You might think that play is only for small children. From games to sports to fun sleepovers, you can find other ways to play. Play brings us laughter, joy, and stress relief. Being playful connects us to others and provides a break from the stresses of everyday life.

Play may change as you grow, but it's important to stay connected to your inner playful nature. The right kind of play happens when you let go of expectations and welcome your inner child. Here are some ideas to get you started:

- Ride a skateboard.
- Throw a ball with a friend.
- Dance alone or with a friend.
- Play with a younger cousin or sibling.
- Make silly photos and videos.

14

Visualize It

Listen carefully to your inner desires. When you visualize your future, you plan for positive change. Take three deep breaths. Inhale positive thoughts and exhale negative thoughts. Close your eyes and ask yourself: *What am I passionate about? What are my strenghts? How do these two things work together?* By visualizing your dreams coming to life, you are taking the first steps toward making it happen.

15

A Mantra for Taking a Pause

"I am not running a race. I choose to enjoy the process and take breaks along the way. When I give myself the space to pause, I can achieve my goals."

Give yourself permission to rest, recharge, and reenergize so you can tackle the challenges life throws at you.

16

~~~

Be Loud

*"There are much more important qualities
to have than a docile disposition."*

—C. J. REDWINE, DEFIANCE

Assert your thoughts. Stand up for your beliefs. Question the answers.

17

~~~

Celebrate Friendship

When you have a good friend in your life, don't wait for a special occasion to celebrate them. Make time for one another. Prioritize having fun together. Celebrate for no reason at all, because good friends are always worth celebrating.

18

Replace Criticism with Curiosity

When we stand on the outside looking in, we tend to think we know better. Instead of criticizing the choices of others, be curious. Ask questions. Dare to wonder if you can learn something new by watching your friends, or even strangers. Curiosity opens our eyes to new possibilities. When we ask more questions, we find new ways to navigate our world.

19

Listen to Yourself

Say this to yourself, either quietly or out loud:

"I am my own unique self. If I strive to look and act like others, I am not being true to me. I have my own look, my own personality, my own strengths, and my own goals. I am me, and I am unique."

20

JANUARY

Positive Thought Bubbles

Positive thinking takes practice. Writing down your thoughts is one way to learn to shift your thinking and talk more positively to yourself.

Fill a piece of paper with blank thought bubbles. Write down all of your strengths and positive attributes in the bubbles.

> What makes you great?
> Are you a great listener for your friends?
> Are you a good problem solver?
> Are you awesome at sports?
> Add anything else you can think of.

Whenever you need a reminder or a boost of positivity, refer back to your thought bubbles and reframe your negative thoughts. Don't ignore your negative thoughts. If you want to work through them, you have to listen to them. What are they trying to tell you? Once you've done that, replace the negative thought with a more positive one.

21

Don't Fear Failure

*"You've got to experience failure to understand
that you can survive it."*

—TINA FEY

Failure teaches you that you won't break every time you bend. You can pick yourself back up and begin again.

22

JANUARY

True Happiness

True happiness occurs when you decide to accept yourself for who you are, be yourself around everyone you meet, and follow your dreams, no matter what anyone else around you is doing.

23

Problem Meter

When you encounter something difficult, put the problem into perspective. Sometimes small problems feel big in the moment, but when you take a step back and look at them from a different point a view, they aren't that bad.

Try using a problem meter to determine how big an obstacle actually is and whether or not you need help solving it. Here's how it works:

1. Draw three squares on a piece of paper.

2. Label the bottom square "Small," the middle square "Medium," and the top square "Big."

3. In each square, write down and categorize the obstacles you are facing. What can you handle on your own? What problems might be better solved with help from others?

4. Next to the top square, draw three horizontal lines. Write the names of three people in your life that you can reach out to if you encounter a big problem.

Categorizing problems and obstacles gives you the emotional space to think about where to begin and what you can do on your own.

24

Create Your Own Happiness

Life is here for you to enjoy right now. Find the people, hobbies, and activities that bring you feelings of happiness and focus on them. You create your own happiness when you find the people and things in your life that spark joy.

25

Share Joy

"The best way to cheer yourself is to try to cheer someone else up."

—MARK TWAIN

If you see someone in need of a boost and you have some joy to share, pay it forward. Helping others, even just by sharing a laugh, leaves everyone feeling a little bit happier.

26

Choose Your Own Path

What would you do differently if you didn't worry about what other people think of you? As a teen, you're constantly being evaluated by teachers, coaches, friends, and even your parents. What if you could turn off the notifications in your brain when those evaluations come in? Who would you be?

Write a list of things *you* want to do. Your list might include activities like learning to knit or trying a new sport. Come up with as many options as you can. Scan your "To Try" list and find one that you can start right away. Give yourself permission to work your way through your own list without worrying about what others might think. Maybe you'll find a hidden talent or a new area of interest!

27

Let Hope Fuel You

Sometimes everything in life will feel as if it's going right. And every now and then, you may feel like everything is going wrong. There will also be times when you feel stuck in between. No matter where you are in your journey to reach your goals, let hope fuel you.

Hope helps you stay focused when things are going well, but it will also help you hang on when life gets overwhelming. Hope is your center, and hope will help you thrive.

28

Dare to Dream

"Without leaps of imagination or dreaming, we lose the excitement of possibilities. Dreaming, after all, is a form of planning."

—GLORIA STEINEM

29

Accept All of You

Accept and embrace all of you. You will experience highs and lows as you go through life; you will become familiar with your strengths and weaknesses. If you only focus on what you think are your best moments or your most important contributions, you will miss out on the parts of you that keep going through the difficult times.

Accept everything that makes you whole. Embrace the good and the bad, the highs and the lows. Celebrate all parts of you.

30
JANUARY

Dwell on the Positive

When positive thoughts enter your mind, hold them close. Slow down and take the time to enjoy them. Life gets busy and thoughts will come and go quickly throughout the day. But when you give yourself a chance to dwell on the good ones, you set yourself up for a positive day.

31
JANUARY

Share Your Happy Moments

One way to savor the happy moments we experience is to stop and share them with others. The more you share good times with those around you, the more others will be inspired to do the same. You can start a chain reaction simply by sharing good news. The next time something good happens:

- Make a phone call
- Send a text
- Share on social media
- Write a letter

Share your good news—and ask others to do the same—to build positivity in your community.

FEBRUARY

1

On Showing Love

*"When we love, we always strive to become better than we are.
When we strive to become better than we are, everything
around us becomes better, too."*

—PAULO COELHO, *THE ALCHEMIST*

2

Be Your Own Friend

Everyone needs supportive people in their lives. But you also need to be there to support yourself.

Cheer yourself on.   Make yourself laugh.
Pick yourself up.   Find your own happiness.

Get to know yourself. You are a great friend to many, but you can also be a wonderful friend to you.

3

A Mantra for Taking Charge of Your Happiness

"I can choose to help myself through difficult times by being kind to myself, reminding myself that I have talents and strengths to share with the world, and by listening and responding to my needs."

Breathe

Even the best days can feel completely overwhelming; positive emotions can be just as overwhelming as negative ones. Learn to reset your emotions by scheduling regular breathing breaks throughout the day.

1. Find a quiet place to sit.

2. Imagine you're smelling a beautiful flower and slowly inhale for a count of four.

3. Hold the image of that flower for another count of four.

4. Now imagine you're blowing out a birthday candle as you exhale for a count of four.

5. Soak in the image of your perfect cake for one last count of four.

Map Your Friendships

Like the ocean waves, friendships may also ebb and flow as you grow and change. This is the nature of friendship. Remember that you have more than one friend in the world and that you are capable of making new ones.

Draw a map of all the places and ways you spend your time. Add the names of the friends you interact with in each space. Perhaps you have some friends at school, but there are others that you see only during sports or after-school activities. You might have a few friends that you know from social media or friends that live in your neighborhood. When you map out your friendships, you will begin to see a visual representation of the many supportive people in your life.

Love Story

Love comes in all shapes and sizes. Family love, friendship love, and romantic love are a few of the forms you might already know. All kinds of love can help you feel comforted and supported as you journey through life, and you may discover that you crave different kinds of love depending on your situation.

Every love has a story, no matter what it looks like. Take the time to write one of your stories of love. Where did it begin? What keeps it strong? What do you value in this person? Come back to your love stories when you need a reminder of the love and support that surrounds you.

Happiness Is an Inside Job

Happiness is a feeling. And like any other feeling, it comes and goes. No one is happy every minute of the day, but you can create a greater degree of happiness by working from the inside out.

Material objects provide moments of happiness, but feeling happy is very different. Create more happiness in your life by getting to know yourself better. Answer the following questions to get you started:

When do I feel the most joy?
What do I enjoy doing when I'm alone?
What do I enjoy doing with friends?
What sparks happiness for me?

8

Smile

"Weird . . . something happens when you smile at people. They smile back."

—RAINA TELGEMEIER, SMILE

Trust that others are looking for happiness, too. When you show positivity, others will return it.

Empathy

em·pa·thy \ 'em-pə-thē \ noun

1. The action of understanding, being aware of, being sensitive to, and vicariously experiencing the feelings, thoughts, and experience of another of either the past or present without having the feelings, thoughts, and experience fully communicated in an objectively explicit manner.

Everyone we meet is fighting their own battles. We all have ups and downs in life, but it's not always obvious when a friend is struggling. Check in on your friends often and respond with empathy. Try to step into their shoes and understand how they're feeling and experiencing life.

When you are empathetic, your friends will see you as a safe space and one who helps others through hard times. They will also be more likely to do the same for you. When empathy is your superpower, you can build strong connections that will last a lifetime.

10

Whenever Possible, Choose Kindness

Conflict happens. You might disagree with your friends, family, or other people in your life, but you don't have to let conflict become wrapped up in anger. When conflict arises, listen to your heart and choose kindness. Before you respond, think carefully about what you want to say. How do you want the conflict to end? Do you want to be right or repair the relationship? If you choose to repair, the best path toward compromise is always kindness.

11
FEBRUARY

On Friendship

"Why did you do all this for me?' he asked. 'I don't deserve it. I've never done anything for you.' 'You have been my friend,' replied Charlotte. 'That in itself is a tremendous thing.'"

—E. B. WHITE, CHARLOTTE'S WEB

12

Friend Love

Books, movies, TV shows, and magazines will lead you to believe that one true love awaits you and will make your life complete. But friend love is just as powerful and sometimes more realistic. We come to love our good friends as family; they are the family that we choose.

A good friend laughs when you need a laugh, holds your hand when you need to cry, distracts you when everything feels like too much, and listens when you need to vent. A good friend is there through good times and bad. A good friend is your other half who holds you up and cheers you on. Friend love is a special kind of love that is unconditional, long-lasting, and worth celebrating.

13
FEBRUARY

~~~

Notes of Gratitude

It can feel good to receive a note of gratitude from someone you care about. But it can feel just as good to send a note of gratitude to someone else. Take some time today to think about the people who play an important role in your life. Think about the following questions and write a few notes of gratitude to the people in your life.

- Why are these people important to you?
- How do they help you?
- What do you value about these relationships?

Expressing gratitude in written form makes you feel happier and nurtures your relationship with the other person. It's a win for everyone!

14
FEBRUARY

Share a Smile

"Let us make one point . . . that we meet each other always with a smile, especially when it is difficult to smile . . . Smile at each other, make time for each other in your family."

—MOTHER TERESA

15
FEBRUARY

Communicate Your Feelings

Learning to own your emotions and express your needs will help you work through problems with friends, family, and everyone else. Try these statements to resolve conflict and open communication:

When . . .   *I need . . .*
I feel . . .   *Please . . .*

16

FEBRUARY

Prioritize Self-Care

If you are tired, overwhelmed, and out of sorts, you won't have the energy for school, activities, friends, or family. You need to learn how to take care of yourself to be able to tackle challenges and reach your goals. Some people assume that self-care looks like long bubble baths or reading for fun, but self-care can be anything that lifts you up. Self-care is a daily practice that serves more than one purpose. Try to make time every day to engage in the following:

- A relaxing activity like a creative outlet, a warm bath, journaling, or meditation
- Healthy eating at regular mealtimes
- An exercise that makes you feel good and happy
- Time with a friend
- Family check-in
- 8 to 10 hours of sleep each night

Creating healthy self-care habits now will help you feel confident and happy as you grow and learn.

17

~

Find the Uplifters

Do your best to surround yourself with people who lift you up, return a smile, extend a hand, take a hand, work together, and care about one another.

The "uplifters" are the people in your life that make the world a supportive place. Be one.

18
FEBRUARY

~

Be Courageous and Kind

"Courage. Kindness. Friendship. Character. These are the qualities that define us as human beings, and propel us, on occasion, to greatness."

—R. J. PALACIO, WONDER

19

Face Your Fear

Fear is a tricky emotion. It tells us what we can and cannot do; telling us to be scared when we should be excited. It limits us and doesn't always tell the truth. Fear is known to send false alarms.

Replace fear with courage. When you experience fear, close your eyes, center yourself with a deep breath, and try to think about times when you've overcome fear in the past. It can even be something small, like learning to ride a bike when you were younger. When you do this, you retrain your brain to focus on your strengths.

Breathe through what makes you feel scared, but have the courage to take risks, try something new, and walk into the unknown. Only then will you know what you're capable of.

20

FEBRUARY

Be Harmonious

The world is full of all kinds of people, places, things, and experiences. Differences are opportunities to learn and grow.

When you are in harmony with everything you encounter, you open yourself to the unknown, which helps you learn about the world around you.

Inner peace doesn't come when we remove all the stress from our lives, but when we choose to live in harmony with everything that comes our way.

21

FEBRUARY

Acceptance

"The older I get, the more I believe that the greatest kindness is acceptance."

—CHRISTINA BAKER KLINE, A PIECE OF THE WORLD

22

~

Write Yourself A Love Letter

Instead of waiting for the perfect letter that tells you all the things you long to hear to arrive in the mail, write it yourself. You know what words of support will pick you up and help you keep going. You know what inspires you to push forward even when something feels impossible.

Take the time to write yourself that letter. Say the things you need to hear. Seal it and keep it someplace safe. When you encounter a day, or week, or month that feels dark and endless, open up that letter. Allow your own words of inspiration to comfort you and give you a boost.

23
FEBRUARY

~

Emotions Are Temporary

We hope that good feelings will last forever, and it can be sad when they end. We also may wish a speedy end to the bad feelings, and can be disappointed when they hang around. We can't control what happens to us, but we can control our response to emotions. Through positive thinking, you can learn to work through all kinds of emotions so that you aren't caught up in the negativity.

Remember: Emotions are temporary. They will come and go, and while some may hang around longer than others, eventually they subside. Embrace the positive ones, work through the negative ones, and remember that you will feel happy again.

24

Your Cup is Always Half Full

When life feels hard, it's tempting to look at your cup as half empty. Hardship and negative emotions have a way of making us feel like everything is pointless. When you start to feel this way, take a pause. Close your eyes, breathe in gratitude, and think about the people and things that fill your cup. Now open your eyes and look again. Your cup is actually half full.

25

A Mantra for Self-Forgiveness

*"I am human, and I make mistakes. I can
learn from the past and try again."*

26

~

Let Go of Resentment

Resentment is like a weed wrapped around your soul. If you don't take steps to get rid of it, it will grow and tighten its grip. But you have the power to let go of resentment by letting go of old hurts and resentful feelings. There's a freedom in letting go and looking forward, and you deserve to experience it.

When you experience feelings of resentment, yell them out loud or write them down. Own them and let them go by saying to yourself: *That can't hurt me anymore. That's over and done.* By stating and releasing your old hurts, you clear up space for new, positive feelings and experiences.

27
FEBRUARY

Live Bravely

"Scared is what you're feeling. Brave is what you're doing."

—EMMA DONOGHUE, ROOM

You can be scared and brave at the same time. All you have to do is keep reaching for your dreams.

28
FEBRUARY

Pursue Your Interests

Your life is yours to live. Your dreams are yours to achieve. You won't find happiness if you only work toward goals other people set for you. True happiness occurs when you figure out who you are, who you want to become, and what you need to do to bridge the gap. This begins with pursuing your own interests. Ask yourself: *What am I passionate about?* Start there and don't stop.

29

Practice Self-Love

If you want others to show you love and acceptance, you must also show yourself love and acceptance. When you criticize yourself, you aren't able to foster the healthy friendships or relationships that you desire.

Learn to accept what you see as your "flaws" by looking at them in a new light. Sometimes simply asking yourself, *What's something good about this?* can help change your perspective. When you practice self-love and accept all parts of yourself, you are able to enter into any relationship with honesty, compassion, and positive energy. This will help your relationships thrive.

MARCH

1

Make the Little Things Big

When life gets busy, we tend to fall into a pattern of running from task to task without stopping to think about all the little things that happen throughout the day. When you're always on the go, you might overlook some great moments: the smile from a teacher meant to give you confidence, the funny story a friend told at the lunch table, or the way you felt when your parent hugged you at the end of a long day.

Our culture of busyness makes us think that we can't stop to savor the little things, but the little things are actually quite important when we take the time to appreciate them: They refuel us, remind us that we are safe and loved, and inspire us to keep going.

Try to slow down and pause for the small moments. Give yourself permission to enjoy a long hug, stretch out a conversation, and laugh a little louder. You can choose to have the little things take up more space, and that will bring you greater happiness.

2
MARCH

~

Beauty Is Everywhere

Take some time to observe the beauty that is life:

The warm sun on your back.
The sound of birds in the sky.
A butterfly's wings beating fast.
The scent of flowers in bloom.
The feel of soft grass under your feet.
Beauty surrounds you wherever you go.

*"When I take a deep breath and allow my senses
to lead me, I am surrounded by nature and
the feeling of peace it has to offer."*

Kind Thoughts Meditation

Intentionally sending kind thoughts to others is a great way to boost overall positivity. When you think good thoughts for others, you tap into empathy and compassion. This increases positive emotions and helps build social connections as you think about your friends and loved ones, even in their absence. Try this meditation:

1. Get into a comfortable position and take three deep breaths.

2. Clear your mind of any clutter as you inhale calm and exhale worry.

3. Picture a friend or loved one as you repeat the following phrases (or similar phrases of your own):

   I hope you are happy.
   I hope you feel loved.
   I hope you are healthy.
   I hope you feel calm.

4. Finish with three more deep breaths as you open your eyes.

In just five minutes, you can find calm and send good thoughts to a friend or loved one in need.

4
MARCH

Be Hopeful

*"We need never be hopeless because we can never be irreparably broken.
We think we are invincible because we are."*

—JOHN GREEN, LOOKING FOR ALASKA

5
MARCH

Peaceful Thoughts

Peaceful thoughts float through our minds like fluffy clouds, keeping us calm and grounded. Sometimes we don't even realize these thoughts are there when we're feeling worry-free.

Tune in to your peaceful thoughts to be mindful of how positive thinking makes you feel. Close your eyes and visualize your thoughts floating on clouds through the bright blue sky. What are your peaceful thoughts telling you?

6

MARCH

Let Go of Guilt

Guilt is an emotion that can eat away at your happiness. It won't make you feel better or solve any inner conflicts, nor does it change a situation.

You can stop feeling guilty by getting your feelings out. Write down any guilty feelings on individual pieces of paper. What contributed to these feelings? Why do these feelings continue to drag you down? Write it all down to release it from your brain, then crumple the papers and throw them away. Let them go; they are behind you now.

7

MARCH

Chain of Positivity

When you think positive thoughts about yourself, you take positive actions to bring those thoughts into reality. It's a chain reaction. What you believe about yourself becomes true when you act on your beliefs.

To start a chain of positive thoughts, close your eyes and begin with one encouraging phrase. You might think to yourself: *I work hard at everything I do.* Try to add more positivity to your chain each day.

8

Rise Above Limitations

When you face a challenge in your life, use your past experiences to work through it. Before you hit the panic button, ground yourself by stating the problem out loud, and then answer the following questions:

- Does this challenge remind you of anything else you've overcome?
- How did you work through that previous challenge?
- What skills did you learn then that you can use now?

When you tap into the tools you already have, you'll find you are prepared to rise above the limitations that sometimes get in your way.

9

Find Your Anchors

"I think that at every stage of living, there are
7 people who matter in your world. They are people
who are inside you. They are people you rely on.
They are people who daily change your life."

—HOLLY GOLDBERG SLOAN, COUNTING BY 7s

Take a moment to think about your anchors. These are the people who are always there for you and keep you grounded, even during hard times. Write their names on a slip of paper and keep it somewhere safe. When you feel lost, look at your list of anchors and remember that you are not alone.

10
MARCH

~~

Listen to Your Body

Believe it or not, your body actually mirrors your inner thoughts. When you experience stress, anxiety, low self-worth, or other feelings of negativity, your body sends signals to remind you to stop and take a break.

It's really important to listen to the cues your body sends so that you can take steps to work through your negative emotions and pivot toward positive thinking. Watch for these stress signals:

- Headaches
- Muscle aches
- Stomachaches
- Difficulty sleeping
- Trouble focusing
- Feeling foggy

When your body sends these signals, use deep breathing to restore calm, take a rest, and talk to someone you trust.

11

The Art of Doing Nothing

Embrace the days when you feel like doing nothing. Those days are necessary to rest, recharge, and prepare to begin again.

12
MARCH

Letter of Self-Forgiveness

We all make mistakes and have feelings of regret from time to time. When we allow these negative feelings to crowd out the positive ones, it can be overwhelming. It's important to forgive yourself for the mistakes you've made. You can't go back in time to change your actions, but you can move forward with a new understanding.

Writing is a great tool for releasing old hurts and finding closure. Write yourself a letter of forgiveness. Pour your feelings into it, show yourself compassion and understanding, and give yourself the love you need to move on. Put this letter in a safe place in your room. You might not need it today or tomorrow, but someday you will. When that day comes, your letter of self-forgiveness will be there to set you free.

13

Deliberate Acts of Kindness

Random acts of kindness are a great way to brighten someone's day, but *deliberate* acts of kindness are also important. When you take the time to consider how you can intentionally spread kindness in your family, your school, and your community, you create positive change.

14

Every Day is a New Opportunity

Today is a new day. Today, you can take the lessons learned yesterday and begin again. When you focus on the gift of today, you take a big step toward reaching your goals.

15
MARCH

~

One Step at A Time

If you want to make positive changes in your life, start with a series of small steps toward a larger goal. If you sprint with long strides, it might be too much, and you may burn yourself out. If you set a slower pace and take smaller steps, you can more easily reach your goal. Creating an action plan at your own pace puts *you* in charge of achieving your goals.

1. What is your goal?

2. Now consider what your finish line looks like.

3. What's one thing that you want to change? Go back to the starting line.

4. What is the first step you need to take?

Map out your small steps from start to finish to make this positive change a reality.

16
MARCH

A Mantra for Change

*"If I want to change my life on the outside, I have to begin
by changing my life on the inside. When I am willing to
change my thinking, I take the first step toward improving my life."*

17
MARCH

Listen to Your Inner Voice

"The one thing that does not abide by majority rule is a person's conscience."

—HARPER LEE, TO KILL A MOCKINGBIRD

18
MARCH

Accept Yourself as You Are

You have your own individual strengths. You are walking your own path to reach your goals. When you compare yourself to others, you might see that you are not on the exact same path as someone else. When you accept yourself as you are and focus on your inner strengths, you begin to see that there is more than one path to success and that you are doing just fine on your path.

19

~~~

The Daily Win

Some days are better than others. Some days, you may feel as if everything is falling into place and things are going your way. Other days, you may feel the opposite. It happens to everyone.

To make your day better, focus on your daily win. Close your eyes and review your day. Find one thing that went well. It doesn't have to be a big thing, just something that felt right. Now open your eyes, stand in front of a mirror, and tell yourself the story of your daily win. Make it detailed. Make it exciting. Pat yourself on the back for finding something positive, even on a hard day. Go to bed knowing that you had at least one win today.

20

~~~

Rewrite Your Story

If you don't like the way your story is being told, write a new ending. You have the power to own your narrative.

21

Find Motivation

Having motivation, or a purpose, helps you stay grounded and focused on a goal. This doesn't have to be big or life-changing. It can be one small daily task that gives you something to pour your energy into, like:

- Making cards for kids in a nearby hospital
- Holding a bake sale to raise money for a cause
- Acting as a homework helper for younger students

When you have a clear purpose in mind, you have something to work toward and look forward to.

22
MARCH

Ask for Help

Everyone needs help sometimes. Think about the people who are there for you. It might be a parent, a friend, a teacher, or a coach. Reach out to your support system when you don't know what to do. Two heads are always better than one.

23
MARCH

Visit Your Happy Place

When you feel sad, angry, or overwhelmed, you can revisit positive memories by anchoring your experiences.

Try to think of a place where you felt calm, happy, and loved. Close your eyes and recreate the space in your mind. Can you remember a time when something fun happened at this place? Replay that memory while you visualize your happy place. Allow yourself to get lost in the memory while breathing in a feeling of calm and happiness.

24
MARCH

Care Greatly

"Of course, they needed to care. It was the meaning of everything."

—LOIS LOWRY, THE GIVER

Caring about your friends, family, and the world around you brings meaning to your life. Dare to care greatly.

25
MARCH

Accomplishment Jar

It can feel good when other people recognize your hard work, but it can feel even better when you learn to recognize your own accomplishments.

Keep an empty jar on your desk. Take a moment each day to add at least one accomplishment to the jar. Did you make a new friend? Write it on a piece of paper and put it in the jar. Did you work through a difficult project? Put it in the jar. When you have a day where you struggle to add something, reach in and read a few of your previous accomplishments out loud. This will give you the boost you need.

26
MARCH

Recharge

Taking time to recharge is productive. When you give your mind what it needs to recover from the normal ups and downs you encounter, you prepare yourself to be more energized, focused, and efficient.

27
MARCH

Enjoy the Little Surprises

When you wake up each day, look for good experiences and open yourself up to pleasant surprises. Search for smiles, accept compliments, and expect positive interactions. When you start the day on a positive note, you'll find that others have good things to share, too.

28
MARCH

Daily Motivation Exercise

Most likely there are various things that motivate you. Some people rely on music to get excited, some are inspired by a positive mantra (or words of wisdom), and others use exercise to get themselves going. Knowing your motivators will help you stay focused, even during a difficult task.

Each day, take five minutes to write down what motivates you. What helps you get started? What has helped you remain on task? Use this list of strategies on days when you don't feel quite as inspired. Keep this list in your desk or backpack so you have your strategies handy when you need them.

29
MARCH

Create an Affirmation Board

Practicing positive affirmations helps you tackle difficult tasks and remain hopeful when you feel overwhelmed. When you say something kind to yourself, you learn to help yourself through the difficult times.

Create a space in your room where you can surround yourself with positive phrases and inspirational quotes. Here are a few to get you started:

I am more than enough.
I love myself exactly how I am.
I can reach my dreams.
My goals are within my own reach.

Now add your own phrases and quotes. Read them out loud when you pass by to remind yourself that you have what it takes to overcome obstacles.

30
MARCH

Find the Light

"I like the night. Without the dark, we'd never see the stars."

—STEPHENIE MEYER, TWILIGHT

31
MARCH

Good Things Journal

You can feel more positive by ending the day thinking of three good things. It might be the scent of fresh-baked cookies or a chat with an old friend. It doesn't have to be huge or life-changing, just something that reminds you that good things happen even on the worst days.

Start a "Good Things" journal. At the end of each day, write down three good things that brightened your day. Fall asleep thinking about the three things that reminded you that life is full of positivity.

APRIL

1

A Mantra for Working Toward Goals

"A work in progress is still progress. I will take small steps each day to get one day closer to reaching my goal."

When you look for the small victories along the way, you see that each effort brings you closer to achieving your goal.

2
APRIL

Just Keep Swimming

When you encounter something difficult, you owe it to yourself to keep going and work through it. You may feel like walking away is the easiest thing to do, but when you remind yourself that you've been through hard times before and you've overcome other obstacles that once felt huge, you'll see that you can keep swimming forward, no matter how stormy the seas may seem.

3
APRIL

Take Action

Anticipating potential problems gives you something to think about, but it doesn't really get you anywhere. Instead of getting lost in anticipatory worry, follow these three steps to sharpen your problem-solving skills:

1. Identify the problem.

2. Brainstorm possible solutions. Use pros and cons to find the best one.

3. Choose a solution and see whether or not it worked.

When you focus on what's actually happening, you can take appropriate actions to solve the problem.

4
APRIL

Extra Care

You can't convince other people to care and empathize as much as you do, but you can care and empathize a little bit extra, and that will make up the difference.

5
APRIL

Get Back Up

"What defines you isn't how many times you crash but the number of times you get back on the bike."

—SARAH DESSEN, ALONG FOR THE RIDE

6

Love Yourself

Sometimes we hear things such as "Don't brag," and we forget that we can and should love ourselves and celebrate our successes. When you are able to identify what you love about yourself, you also find your character strengths. You can be good at a lot of things, but having defined character strengths (like listening skills, empathizing with others, making people laugh, etc.) shapes who you are from the inside out.

Take a moment to consider what you really love about yourself. Who are you? If you were to brag about your inner strengths, what would it sound like? Try finishing these sentences:

I love that I am . . .
I love that I can . . .
I love that people come to me for . . .

7
APROL

A Mantra for Self-Acceptance

"I accept and love the way I look and who I am.
I don't need to compare myself to anyone else."

8
APRIL

Give Yourself Time to Recharge

Take a break today. You probably have a lot on your plate right now, and you may feel like you're under pressure most of the time. It's nearly impossible to do your best when you can't get enough rest. Everyone needs a little bit of downtime every day. Set an alert on your phone to drop everything and rest at some point during the day. Read a magazine, listen to music, or simply close your eyes and give yourself a chance to recharge.

Fresh Start

Each morning when you wake up, give yourself the gift of a fresh start. Before you even get out of bed, follow these steps:

1. Take three deep breaths.
2. Forgive yourself for yesterday's mistakes.
3. Think about how you want your day to go.
4. Run through your gratitude list.
5. Smile.

Starting your day this way sets a positive tone for today and every day.

10
APRIL

Replace Questions with Statements

Everyone thinks about how they measure up to others. We all do it. Sometimes we can be our biggest critics when we think others have more, do more, or experience greater success. One way to reframe this kind of thinking is to replace the questions we ask ourselves with actual facts. For example, instead of *Am I good enough?* try *I am fine just the way I am.*

11
APRIL

Discover Your Gift

"Maybe, I am thinking, there is something hidden
like this, in all of us. A small gift from the
universe waiting to be discovered."

—JACQUELINE WOODSON, *BROWN GIRL DREAMING*

Listen to your inner dreams to discover your own hidden gift.

12
APRIL

~~~

Take Control of Your Choices

"I know you may feel so far that circumstances have directed your path, but right now I want you to know that you do have a choice."

—LARRY ITEJERE, THE SILVER ARROW

13
APRIL

~~~

Surround Yourself with Positive People

When you spend time with energetic, positive people, you get a boost of positive energy. When you spend too much time with people who complain or focus on the negative, you might feel drained. Surround yourself with people who make you feel energized, empowered, and hopeful.

14
APABIL

Get Moving!

Research shows that exercise improves your self-esteem. If team sports aren't your thing, don't worry. Grab a friend and find a fun class to take or download a fitness app to use together. YouTube also has tons of fun fitness videos for people of all ages to help make exercise fun.

15
APABIL

Share a Laugh

Looking for the funny moments can help you get through the difficult ones. Hold on to those moments to cheer yourself up when you need it, or, even better, text it to a friend to cheer someone else up right away. Sharing a laugh with a friend is always a great way to feel happy.

16

Practice Self-Compassion

Self-doubt is the thief of joy. When we question our choices, abilities, and intentions every step of the way, we live in a state of self-judgment. It may feel like you're always telling yourself that you're not good enough.

Self-compassion involves having a positive attitude and showing kindness toward ourselves. It means accepting your mistakes and giving yourself a break when things don't actually go as planned. Showing self-compassion means appreciating the ups and downs of life. There's no one way to practice self-compassion, but try these tips to get started:

- Practice daily mindfulness to increase your awareness of your inner thoughts and feelings.
- Respond to yourself as you would to a friend when something isn't going well.
- Practice acceptance statements like *It's okay that I'm upset*, or, *One mistake isn't life-changing*.
- Write yourself a note each day to focus on what's right in your world.

17

APRIL

~

Flip the Script

You will make mistakes and confront failure. Everyone does; it's part of growing up. But failure doesn't have to drag you down or make you feel embarrassed. You can flip it around into something positive.

1. Grab an index card and write down one failure, mistake, or disappointment that occurred today.

2. Think about why it might have happened.

3. Flip the card over and write down what you can do next time to avoid that same misstep.

For example: If one side says, "I failed my Spanish test," the other side might read, "I'll make flash cards and ask my teacher for extra help."

18
APRIL

~

Jump In!

When you sit around thinking about the pros and cons of trying something new, you may end up spending too much emotional energy on evaluating the situation. This can zap you of the energy you need to get out there and try something new. Instead of overthinking, ask yourself a few questions:

Does it sound fun?
Does it sound interesting?
Is it safe?
Will I learn something new?

If you answered "yes" to these questions, jump in! Try something different and see how it goes. Even if you don't love it, you will learn something new about yourself!

19

Create a Life List

We all have dreams about what we hope for in our lives. Dreaming about what we want to happen is a great way to think about a positive future.

Take it one step further by starting a running "Life List" that includes your hopes and dreams for the present and the future. This list can include things you hope to learn, places you want to visit, goals you want to accomplish, and fun things you want to do. Add to this list when new dreams and ideas pop into your head. Pin it up in your room so that you see it often. Find one thing on the list that you can actually begin working toward right away. Circle it. What's the first step you need to take to make this dream come true? If you can dream it, you can find a way to do it.

20
APRIL

~

Create a Bowl of Gratitude

Practicing gratitude can help you focus on the great things that life has to offer. The trouble is that it can be hard to keep the positive things front and center; the list may go missing or your mind might be racing with other thoughts during the day. A bowl of gratitude can change that. Here's what you do:

1. Collect some stones around your neighborhood.

2. Wash and dry the stones to remove any dust and dirt.

3. Paint one side of each stone white or another light color, so you can read text.

4. Use a permanent marker to write down one person or thing that you are grateful for on each rock.

5. Place them in a bowl or vase and put it on your desk or nightstand.

6. When you need positive energy, pull out a rock, read it, and picture that person or thing in your mind.

21
APRIL

Do Something Special

Have you ever secretly decorated a friend's locker and then watched from down the hall as they discovered the surprise? When you do kind things for other people, everyone feels happier as a result.

22
APRIL

Good Thoughts are Beautiful

"A person who has good thoughts cannot ever be ugly. You can have a wonky nose and a crooked mouth and a double chin and stick-out teeth, but if you have good thoughts they will shine out of your face like sunbeams and you will always look lovely."

—ROALD DAHL, *THE TWITS*

23

APRIL

Be Different

Sometimes we fear the word "different" because it might mean not fitting in. To fit in, we often feel like we have to act or look like someone else.

   If you try to squeeze yourself into a certain box just to fit the mold of what's accepted in your school, you might lose your true self in the process. It takes courage to stand out and be different, so don't be afraid. Learn from your friends, but teach them by letting your personality shine.

24

APRIL

Embrace What Is

"We can what-if ourselves to death . . . But what-if never does anybody any good. All any of us ever have . . . is one thing, and we better make the most of it while we can: What is."

—MIKE LUPICA, MIRACLE ON 49TH STREET

25

Wall of Pride

What are you proud of today? Chances are your life feels busy most of the time, and that can make it difficult to slow down and think about the great things you accomplish each day. Create a wall of pride by taking a few moments at the end of the day to write your proud moments on sticky notes. Examples might include:

I'm proud of my hard work on my English essay.
I'm proud of my teamwork during my game.
I'm proud of my friend for scoring a goal.

Being proud doesn't have to be just about you. You can express pride for your friends, siblings, parents, and any other important people in your life. When you write these daily expressions of pride and stick them to a wall or your bedroom door, you remind yourself daily that even when things get hard, there is always something to be proud of.

26
APRIL

~

Happiness

Happiness isn't something that happens to you; it's a state of being. It's a choice you make every day. Work through the hard stuff and focus on the good stuff.

27
APRIL

~

I AM

You don't have to be a poet to write something that makes you feel good. Try this exercise to remind yourself that you are really great just the way you are. Each line begins with the words "I AM." That's it. That's the only rule. Who are you? Start writing to find out! For example:

I AM a good friend. I check in on my friends when they have a bad day.
I AM a hard worker. I give it my all every single day.
I AM a listener. I take time to be there when someone needs an ear.
I AM funny. I like to make people smile.

28
APRIL

I Know Me Best

We all tend to worry about the "invisible audience," that feeling like you're always being watched and judged, even when you're not.

Turn away from the invisible audience. You know who you are and what gifts you bring to the world. Stand tall and remember that you are the only you out there, and you are worth knowing.

29
APRIL

You Don't Have to Be Loud to Be Seen

Some people are naturally more outspoken than others, and that's okay. It takes all kinds of people to make the world a wonderful place.

If you always speak up, keep it up! Use your strong voice to stand up for others. But if you are quiet and like to observe, you do not have to feel invisible. Your kindness and ideas will shine through when you share with others in any way that feels right to you. Smile at someone who looks sad, send a message to connect with someone, or be the listener who helps others work through ideas.

30
APRIL

Color Your World

Remember when you were little, and it was easy to get your feelings out because you could scream and cry no matter where you were? As you get older, it may not always be so easy to release emotions, but tapping into your inner child can actually help you.

Grab a piece of paper and colorful markers or whatever you have on hand. Think of a color that best represents each of your feelings right now. Go ahead and scribble out each feeling on the paper, using each of the colors to represent your many feelings. Don't worry about coloring in any specific pattern; the messier, the better. Let your colors out!

The act of scribbling releases tension, and thinking through each emotion as you switch colors actually helps you work through them internally. Now, take a deep breath and do something that makes you feel calm.

MAY

1

MAY

—

Test Your Thinking

Avoiding negative thoughts isn't easy. Sometimes you might feel like you're bombarded with negative thoughts throughout the day.

You can test your negative thinking by challenging each thought as it comes. First, recognize the negative thought, then rate how true it is on a scale of 1 to 10. Find what might be supporting evidence for your thought. Now challenge the thought. Finally, revisit your rating. How true is the thought now? Here's an example of how this will work:

> **Thought:** *I'm failing science class.*
> **Rating:** On a scale of 1 to 10, how true is this thought? — 8
> **What supports this thought?** *I failed a pop quiz today.*
> **Challenging thought:** *One pop quiz does not affect my grade that much. I can make it up.*
> **Rating:** From 1 to 10, how true is the original thought now? — 3

When you learn to break down your negative thoughts and challenge them with positive responses, you begin to change your thought patterns.

2
MAY

Find Your Own Thing

Friends tend to travel in groups, and sometimes that means joining clubs or doing other things you normally wouldn't, just to be with your friends. Remember: You can be part of your group *and* do your own thing. Listen to your inner voice to guide you toward your own interests. That's how you'll truly shine.

3
MAY

Inside Out

It's okay to keep some of your thoughts and feelings on the inside, but there may be some that you want to share with your friends and family. We tend to keep our thoughts inside for various reasons, such as privacy or fear of being judged or criticized. Think about your inner thoughts and feelings. Why are you holding them in? Now think of one supportive person in your life who you feel comfortable sharing one of these thoughts with. Practice saying it out loud to yourself first, then reach out to that person. You may find relief by trusting someone with your inside thoughts.

4
MAY

Sadness is Temporary

"In this life, rain's gonna fall, but the sun will shine again."

—KWAME ALEXANDER, REBOUND

5
MAY

Celebrate Along the Way

You don't need a huge milestone, like a graduation, to celebrate your hard work. In fact, when you learn to celebrate your small victories along the way, you may find that you feel happier, and your self-confidence will soar.

It's easy to get caught up in what we need to do to cross the finish line, but we often forget that making it to the end means a long list of little victories along the way. Celebrate every little victory to keep up the positive vibes and remind yourself that you are working hard.

6
MAY

—

Memory Lane

Happy memories flood us with feelings of joy. When we allow ourselves to remember the good times, we can get in touch with the people, places, and things that brought us happiness in the past.

Take a trip down memory lane today. Close your eyes, clear your mind, and use your senses:

> **Hear:** *What familiar sounds in this memory make me feel happy?*
> **Smell:** *What can I smell that reminds me of good times?*
> **Touch:** *Do I feel warm and cozy, or cool and free?*
> **Taste:** *Is there something delicious in my memory, like an ice-cream cone on a hot summer day?*
> **See:** *What do I see? What colors are in the scenery that trigger positive feelings?*

When you remember with your senses, mindfulness helps you experience the memory.

7
MAY

~

Assume Good Things Will Come

If you assume that life is working against you, you'll have no problem finding any issue that you come across. But if you change your thinking and assume that things are actually working *for* you (even on the hard days), you will discover the solutions.

8
MAY

~

A Simple Reminder

Sometimes it is important to remember:

Bad days happen.
You don't have to be perfect.
Asking for help is a sign of strength.
Small steps are important steps.
Tomorrow is a new day.

Take Risks

*"If you don't fall, how are you going to know
what getting up feels like?"*

—STEPHEN CURRY

Make a list of three to five things you want to try (e.g., a new sport, a fashion design class, etc.) but keep putting off because you're worried you won't be good enough. Circle the one that you want to do the most. What do you have to do to make it a reality? Create a list of steps you need to take to go for it. Take the risk and see where it leads you.

10

Design Your Day

It can often feel like we don't have any control over our lives; some days may feel like they are only made up of things that happen to us. When you're a teen, life can feel like an endless cycle of doing what's expected of you.

But you are not a passive player in your life. You get to design your own day, every day. What's important to know is that how you respond to everything you encounter on any given day is a choice. By taking the time to think through your responses to the challenges you face, you give yourself the opportunity to find a positive spin or silver lining. You can work through hard things if you slow down and think empowering thoughts. Choosing how you respond puts you back in control.

What do you want today to look like? Design your day based on what you want and hope to accomplish.

11

MAY

Positive Thoughts

Focus on the positive things in your life right now by finishing these sentences:

> *Today I am happy because . . .*
> *I often look forward to . . .*
> *Something I enjoy doing is . . .*
> *I enjoy hanging out with . . .*
> *Something I dream about is . . .*
> *I get my strength from . . .*

Spend 5 to 10 minutes a day finishing these sentences to begin refocusing on the good things in life.

12
MAY

Cheer Yourself On!

When you replace your inner critic with an inner cheerleader, you learn to give yourself praise and positive responses for your hard work. The next time your inner critic starts to judge you, take a deep, cleansing breath and say something positive about yourself. Be your own cheerleader.

13
MAY

Different is Good

"When you're different, sometimes you don't see the millions of people who accept you for what you are. All you notice is the one person who doesn't."

—JODI PICOULT, CHANGE OF HEART

14

Grade Yourself

If you feel like you're under a microscope every single day, you're not alone. Whether it's grades in school, a coach making decisions about the starting lineup, or earning a part in the musical, it may seem like you're being judged or evaluated by everyone. It's hard to stop worrying about judgment when it's happening all around you.

Take back some of your power by grading yourself. You might not always earn the grade you think you deserve in school or get the lead role in the play, but you can evaluate how hard you're working and be proud of that work.

On a scale of 1 to 10, with 10 being "outstanding," how would you grade yourself today? Use the following prompts to grade yourself on what really matters.

- Showed kindness to others:
- Worked hard:
- Asked for help:
- Helped someone else:
- Stayed positive:

15
MAY

Search for Kindness

The world is full of kind people wanting to help those in need. When you open your eyes to the kindness and compassion around you, you'll find that good always wins over bad.

16
MAY

Bravery Map

Scenes from TV and movies can make us think that being brave means taking heroic action, but that's not true. Being brave means knowing that something is scary or overwhelming, but doing it anyway. It means working through the hard feelings and trying again.

Think back on your childhood. From the time you were little until now, what are some brave things that you did? The first day of school can feel very brave. Hospital visits are also brave. Think about all of your brave acts, big and small, and map them out. When you're done, look over your map and feel proud. What this map shows you is that you are brave.

17
MAY

You Are the Best You

"You are magnificent beyond measure, perfect in your imperfections, and wonderfully made."

—ABIOLA ABRAMS, *THE SACRED BOMBSHELL HANDBOOK OF SELF-LOVE*

18
MAY

You Will Achieve Your Dreams

The road to your own success in life isn't always smooth. In fact, it's often very crooked and filled with unexpected challenges. Sometimes it may feel like you're cruising along and everything is going well, and other times it may feel like you're stuck.

Your dreams will change along the way, and life might not turn out exactly as planned, but you will get there. You will thrive in this world. You will create your happy ending.

19
MAY

A Mantra for Lifelong Learning

"I am always learning more about who I am and what matters to me.
I know that I can change as I grow."

20
MAY

Branch Out

Tree branches and vines reach for the sunlight when left alone to grow; they wrap themselves around other trees and vines, and they very rarely stay put. Their roots are firm in the ground, but they can also explore the world around them.

We tend to get stuck in our own patterns. You sit with the same people, go to the same classes, follow the same routine, and stick close to your roots. It's great to know where your roots are planted, but it's also important to branch out. Try new things, meet new people, and expand your routines. When you branch out, you welcome change and adventure. This is how you grow, develop, and move forward.

21
MAY

Create Healthy Boundaries

"No" is a complete sentence. Teens sometimes struggle to set boundaries because it may seem like the role of the adult. But you can learn to create your own healthy boundaries.

Sometimes boundaries refer to physical touch, such as "No, I don't want a hug," or "No, I don't want your arm around me." Other times, boundaries refer to something emotional, like: "No, I can't stay on the phone for another hour," or "No, I don't want to get involved in your argument."

Boundaries help you:

- Establish physical safety.
- Care for your emotions.
- Prioritize your health needs.
- Give you both emotional and physical space from others.

When you become comfortable with saying "no," you begin to learn to set your own boundaries.

22
MAY
~

Find Your Crew

One of the biggest pitfalls of the teen years can be joining a group just for the sake of belonging. You don't need a group of strangers to make you feel like you're worth knowing. What you need is a group of friends who will stand by you, no matter what comes your way.

Try out all kinds of friends until you find the group (big or small) that really works for you.

23
MAY
~

You Are Enough

You will never be perfect. None of us are. Here's a big secret about this life you're living: You will always be enough.

24
MAY

Don't Cry Alone

The teen years can feel lonely. There's so much pressure to succeed that it might feel hard to connect and ask for help. Don't go it alone. Everyone struggles at times. When you need a good cry, find a friend who won't judge you, and cry together.

25
MAY

You Have What It Takes

One of the most difficult aspects of being a teen is learning to trust your instincts. People have been telling you what to do your entire life. But you have what it takes to thrive in the world. You have good instincts. You know how to solve problems and work through hard feelings. All you have to do is listen to that little voice inside of you that's trying so hard to be heard. Turn down the volume of the people around you who claim to have all the answers and turn up the volume of your inner voice. This is how you learn to trust yourself.

26
MAY

Anger is Heavy

Anger is a very normal human emotion. Everyone can get angry for a variety of reasons. But anger is a heavy burden to carry around. If you don't let it out, it will wear you down. Some people need time alone to release tension; some people need time for physical activity. The best way to find out what works for you is to try a bunch of different techniques. You could:

- Write it down.
- Yell it into a pillow.
- Squeeze a stress ball.
- Get some exercise.

When you find a strategy that helps you work through your anger, you become free of the heavy burden of carrying around old wounds.

27

~~~

Practice Compassion

When times are tough, we look to others for support and help. But you could also be the helper, the support for someone else. Listen with compassion and show others that you care.

28
MAY

~~~

Don't Compare

Admire others for their strength and determination, but don't compare yourself to anyone else. Your beginning might be someone else's middle. Look for inspiration from those slightly ahead of you in a similar goal, but give yourself the gift of time to learn at a pace that works for you.

29

Happiness Takes Time

It's unreasonable to expect that you will feel happy every minute of every day. You will encounter hard situations that make you feel sad, overwhelmed, angry, or hurt. Happiness takes time and commitment. You have to work at it. Each day:

- Think about your strengths.
- Identify something that made you happy.
- Talk about one obstacle that you had to overcome.
- Name one person who supported you.

When you take time each day to do this, you practice happiness.

30
MAY

~

Run Toward Your Future

"You can't run away from who you are, but what you can do is run toward who you want to be."

—JASON REYNOLDS, GHOST

31
MAY

~

Start Small

A skyscraper cannot be built in a single day. You have to create a blueprint, make a plan, and break it down into a thousand little steps.

It's the same with reaching your personal goals. Lay the foundation and keep going, brick by brick. Start small. Take a thought and plan around it. Build it up as you reach your milestones within the goal.

For example, if your goal is to make the basketball team, start by working on your fundamentals, find the shots that need correcting, and commit to a little bit of practice every day.

JUNE

1

JUNE

I Can Do It!

If something feels difficult, or a task seems so big that you don't know where to start, that's okay. We all feel that way at times. The trick is to reframe your thoughts with *I can* instead of *I can't*.

When your thoughts come from a place of self-doubt, you start to think things like *This is too hard*, or *This is impossible*. When you tap into *I can* thinking, you begin the process of breaking the overwhelming task into something manageable. Try it now:

> *I can make a plan to tackle this project.*
> *I can ask for help if I need it.*
> *I can take my time and take breaks, so I don't feel overwhelmed.*
> *I can do this!*

2

Hold Tight to Hope

"So many miracles have not yet happened."

**—KATE DICAMILLO, FLORA & ULYSSES:
THE ILLUMINATED ADVENTURES**

3

Be Patient

Maybe you feel stuck right now. It happens sometimes. Answers will come to you, and you will find the right direction. You might experience a few failures before you find that direction, but with patience and time, you will find your way.

—BARACK OBAMA

What You Can Control

There's a lot you can't control in life, and that can be frustrating. But if you only focus on what you can't control, you might miss out on what you do have control over. It's a lot more than you think. Examples include:

- Your physical boundaries
- Your emotional boundaries
- How you respond to others
- How hard you work
- How you cope with mistakes and setbacks
- How you treat others
- The steps you take to reach your goals

Be the Change

"Change will not come if we wait for some other person, or if we wait for some other time. We are the ones we've been waiting for. We are the change that we seek."

—BARACK OBAMA

Work for Your Friendships

Sometimes a friend can be a best friend for a while, but then they fade to make room for new ones. We all change and grow, but it takes work to keep your friendships intact.

Your friends are your support, but they are also a source of fun and adventure. You can make room for new friends while still holding tight to old ones. You can work through arguments and conflict and come out with a better friendship as a result.

7

A Mantra for Positive Self-Talk

"I talk to myself in a positive way. If I catch myself using negative or dismissive words, I will change them."

8

Replace Need with Have

When you encounter an obstacle in your path, instead of thinking, *What do I need to get through this?* ask yourself, *What do I already have that can get me through this?* Chances are, you have what it takes to get through the hard stuff.

Your Input Matters

Young people may sometimes feel dismissed by adults. When this happens, it might be tempting to yell or storm off, but that breaks down communication. The key to working through a tough conversation so that you feel heard is to stay calm and use your words carefully.

Here are some examples:

> "Can we talk more about this? I feel like I have some good ideas, but I need time to think about it."
> "I've been thinking a lot about this, and I'm hoping . . ."
> "I think I know how we can meet in the middle on this."

Your ideas are important, and your input matters. Keep calm and be open to feedback. More often than not, compromise can help you assert your ideas.

10

Notice the Little Things

Take a mindful walk around your neighborhood and pay attention to the little things you encounter. Stop to smell a beautiful flower; watch a bird fly through the sky; listen to the sound of the leaves rustling in the wind. The little things remind us that good things are always around, even when we feel down.

11

On Optimism

"One of the things I learned the hard way was that it doesn't pay to get discouraged. Keeping busy and making optimism a way of life can restore your faith in yourself."

—LUCILLE BALL

12
JUNE

Take Control of Your Attitude

When you decide to take control of your attitude, you take control of your life. The way you accept and give feedback, work with others, and approach problems all play a role in developing a positive attitude. Help yourself take control of your attitude by:

- Listening more than you talk.
- Using deep breathing to stay calm.
- Asking others for their input.
- Being a problem solver not a problem creator.

13
JUNE

Clear Your Mind

It's nearly impossible to live a positive life with a negative mind. Clear your mind of the negative clutter that drags you down. Own your thoughts, cope with them, and let your thoughts float away.

14
JUNE

Blessings

Count your blessings, not your problems. Focusing on your problems can make you feel discouraged. Focusing on the blessings of others can lead to jealousy. Look inward and count your own blessings to feel grateful for where you are and what you have.

15
JUNE

Finding Rainbows

It can be fun to find rainbows after a storm. Rainbows are often associated with hope for better times ahead. The important thing about rainbows, though, is what creates them: sunshine *and* rain.

Instead of running from the stormy days, try waiting out the rain to see what emerges when the sun returns. We all have moments of both rain and sunshine in our lives. You can't always block the rain to create the perfect life, but you can enjoy the rainbow after you get through the hard times.

16
JUNE

Be an Encourager

When you encourage your friends and family members, you show them that you are with them and there to help. Cheering others on communicates friendship and support. We all need people in our lives who lift us up and encourage us to keep going. When you do this for others, they will do the same for you. Here are a few ways that you can be there for other people in your life:

- Make eye contact (put down your phone) when friends seek you out.
- Practice empathic listening. Respond with "That sounds hard. How can I help?"
- Encourage your friends to keep trying.
- Support your friends when tackling challenges.
- Cheer your friends on.

17
JUNE

Find Beauty in the Ordinary

Life is full of beauty; it's up to you to take the time to notice it. Watch the sun rise and set, smell the rain, run through the grass with bare feet, listen to laughter, enjoy the feeling of the cold ocean on a hot day. Notice the beauty your world has to offer.

18
JUNE

Trust Yourself

The more you believe in yourself, the more you learn to trust yourself. The more you trust yourself, the less you need praise and acceptance from others. Trust that you have what it takes to work through the hard stuff, reach your goals, make good friends, love with all your heart, and find your way to happiness.

19

Believe in Magic

Remember when you were a child and believed in magic? Close your eyes and take a moment to listen to your inner child. How does it feel when you let the magic guide you?

When you open your eyes, rethink magic. Magic can be found in the ordinary when you take the time to look. When sun hits the water from the hose at just the right angle, a rainbow appears. When a hummingbird hovers just near your eyeline, it's breathtaking. Find the magic in the ordinary and remember them when you're feeling blue.

20

Set Happy Goals

If you're happy and you know it, keep going. Then repeat. Do more of what makes you happy. So many of us feel the relentless pressure to succeed right now, but the truth is that the most successful people listen to their inner dreams and follow them. When you are happy, you will reach (or perhaps even surpass) your goals.

21
JUNE

Make Positive Choices

You can't always change the circumstances in your life that feel hard or overwhelming, but you can make small choices that increase your happiness. You can choose:

To surround yourself with positive people.
To learn coping skills to work through stress.
To find the helpers in your community.
To use social media in a positive way.
To put positive energy into the world.

22
JUNE

You Deserve Happiness

You deserve to be happy. You deserve to have good friends. You deserve to laugh, love, and feel pride. You are doing your best, and you deserve good things.

23
JUNE

Favorite Things Collage

Creating a collage can be a great way to relax when you need a break, and it can inspire you when you need a positive boost. Make a "Favorite Things" collage to help refocus your thoughts on things and ideas that make you feel good. Fill it with anything you like: your favorite activities, foods, places you've been or want to visit, fashions, sports, and anything else that makes you smile. When you're done, hang your collage in your room so you can get lost in your favorite things when you need a pick-me-up.

24
JUNE

Go for It

It's natural to wonder about whether or not you're *ready* to tackle a new challenge. Everyone experiences uncertainty or self-doubt at times. When you start wondering whether or not you can do something, remember this: You are as ready as you'll ever be. If you're always preparing, you'll never take a chance. Go for it. Bet on yourself and tackle that challenge.

25
JUNE

Get Started

*"The miracle isn't that I finished. The miracle
is that I had the courage to start."*

**—JOHN BINGHAM, *NO NEED FOR SPEED: A BEGINNER'S
GUIDE TO THE JOY OF RUNNING***

Thinking about starting won't actually get you started. Make a plan.
Break it down into daily goals. Start today.

26
JUNE

Listen to the Silence

It is amazing how much you can learn from silence, and how much it can
energize you. Power down, find a relaxing space to stretch out, listen to
the silence. Breathe, relax, and unwind.

27

Square Breathing

It's natural to feel anxious or frustrated at times. It makes sense; especially when you have a lot on your plate. When you learn how to breathe through heated emotions, you can calm down your entire body and refocus.

Square breathing is a great way to calm yourself, and you can even do it while sitting at your desk or in a group—no one will notice! To get started:

1. Open the palm of one hand and give it a stretch.

2. With your other hand, begin to draw a square in your outstretched hand while taking a deep breath.

3. Inhale slowly and trace up one side for a count of four.

4. Hold your breath and trace across the top for a count of four.

5. Exhale and trace down the other side for a count of four.

6. Hold while you trace across the bottom for four to complete the square.

7. Repeat until you feel calm.

28
JUNE

~

Take Your Time

Your goals are not meant to be completed in one day. Working on improving your thinking takes time and practice. Chip away at it little by little. You may encounter some setbacks here and there, but that's to be expected. Take your time and focus on your small steps toward change.

29
JUNE

~

Laugh

"Laughter is poison to fear."

—GEORGE R. R. MARTIN, A GAME OF THRONES

Let laughter and humor chase away fears and self-doubt. When you laugh, you let your feelings out.

Kindness Splash

It feels good to hear something nice about yourself, but you shouldn't wait around for others to give you the kindness you want and deserve. Give yourself a splash of kindness to remind yourself how great you are:

1. Grab a piece of paper or create a new note in your phone.

2. Set a timer for three minutes.

3. Spend the time filling your page with kind thoughts and words about you.

4. When the timer goes off, look over the list and feel a boost of kindness and purpose.

5. Revisit your list when you feel the stress of a difficult day.

JULY

1

JULY

Look How Far You've Come

Take a moment to look back at the progress you've made this year. Enjoy a deep breath as you think about the obstacles you've conquered, the goals you continue to work toward, and the positive things that have happened along the way. Celebrate this moment. Be proud of you.

2

JULY

Quiet is a Gift

"Quiet people have the loudest minds."

—STEPHEN HAWKING

Embrace the quiet. Open yourself up and listen to what your mind is trying to tell you.

134

3

~

Today Is Your Day

It's easy to get caught up in your "woulds," "shoulds," and "coulds." There's almost always something you would have, should have, or could have done differently. Life can feel that way sometimes, especially when you're young. But that is yesterday's thinking.

It's time to learn how to tap into today thinking. Try these thoughts to help you take a positive approach every day:

Today I can be positive by . . .
When something is hard, I will . . .
If I need help, I can ask . . .
When I make a mistake, I can . . .

Today is your day to practice positive thinking. You have what it takes to begin again.

4

JULY

Reset Your Goals

The summer is a good time to look at your personal goals and think about any changes you want to make. Maybe you already met a few of your goals, or perhaps your goals moved in a different direction. If you have your personal goals written down, take them out and evaluate them. Ask yourself these questions:

- *Did I meet this goal?*
- *If not, what do I have to do to meet this goal?*
- *Does this goal need an adjustment to reflect my life right now?*
- *What smaller benchmarks can I create to work toward this goal?*

If you don't have any goals written down, don't sweat it. Take a few moments to think about one thing you want to achieve. Write it down. Now think of two to three steps that are necessary to reach this goal. Write them down. Those are your benchmarks. Now you have a new goal to focus on starting today.

5
JULY

Share Positive Energy

When you feel a burst of positive energy, share it with someone you care about, like your best friend or a family member. Happiness and positivity have a way of spreading, and sometimes all it takes is sharing the good parts of your day with someone else and listening when they have good things to share with you.

6
JULY

Sunshine

"There is strange comfort in knowing that no matter what happens today, the Sun will rise again tomorrow."

—AARON LAURITSEN, 100 DAYS DRIVE: THE GREAT NORTH AMERICAN ROAD TRIP

7

JULY

A Mantra for Honoring Your Feelings

"I honor all of my feelings because they help me deal with experiences. On days when I experience positive feelings, I allow myself to enjoy them. On days when negative feelings get me down, I give myself permission to experience those emotions, because all of my feelings teach me important lessons."

8

JULY

Small Steps Add Up

The going will get tough sometimes, but that's okay. You have what it takes to keep going. When you feel like you can't keep running through the storm, slow down and take smaller steps. Put one foot in front of the other and just keep going. Small steps add up to big steps when you put them all together.

Live for Today

With stress and pressure coming at you from so many angles, it's normal to focus only on what you need to do to get to the next milestone. The teen years can feel like a slow race to graduation. If you're always thinking about what comes next, you might miss out on the great moments happening today.

Instead of waking up thinking about what tasks you need to complete in the next week, month, or year, take a deep cleansing breath and think about what's in store for today.

What are you looking forward to?
What do you need to make today a good day?

Appreciate the small moments, let go of your stress, connect with people who make you feel good, and get busy enjoying today.

10

JULY

The Gift of Patience

When you are patient, you will find your best friends, make your dreams come true, work through hard things at your own pace, and find your passion. With patience, you give yourself time to learn and grow at your own pace.

11

JULY

Find Your Purpose

Discovering your purpose is how you build self-esteem. You don't have to be the same as all your friends or fit some perfect mold defined by others. Figure out who you are and how you want to bring your strengths to the world. That's purpose. Knowing your purpose brings meaning to your life and helps you establish your goals.

Spend five minutes each day journaling your dreams, hopes, and desires, as well as your obstacles and challenges. Focus on the meaning beneath these thoughts. Somewhere in there, you'll find your true purpose.

12

~~~

Notice Your Shifts

It's completely normal to experience shifting emotions throughout the day, especially as a teen. You might wake up full of optimism and ready to tackle the day only to be derailed by an argument with your parents that leaves you feeling down. It happens.

When you take note of your shifts and track what triggers them, you can better anticipate your moods and plan accordingly. An easy way to do this is to keep a "Trigger Tracker" in the note-taking app on your mobile phone.

1. Start by assigning colors to emotions (e.g., red for mad, green for calm, or yellow for happy).

2. Once you have your color code down, take a few minutes each day to observe what's happening when your mood shifts. For example, you might jot down, "Calm–no homework."

A trigger tracker not only helps you navigate your ups and downs by evaluating what kinds of experiences affect your moods, but it will also help you discover patterns. If you know how certain things affect you, you can make positive choices to improve the outcome.

13
JULY

Take a Break Today

You don't need to plan a fancy vacation to enjoy a vacation day. Think about what makes you feel calm and happy when you have a day off. Do you like picnics? Grab a friend, pack a lunch, and go for a hike. What about a lazy day in the sun? Make your backyard into your own personal beach. You deserve a break today. Take it.

14
JULY

Share Your Thoughts

When you share your thoughts and feelings with someone, you open the door to trust and connection. It can be hard to take that first step toward opening yourself up to someone else, but when you do, you'll find that you are never truly alone.

Reach out to a trusted friend or family member. If you're not sure how to get started, simply say, "I want to talk to you about something, but I don't know where to begin."

15

JULY

Take a Leap

*"He who leaps for the sky may fall,
it's true. But he may also fly."*

—LAUREN OLIVER, DELIRIUM

16

JULY

Create

You don't have to identify as an artist, writer, or musician to be creative. When you unleash any kind of creative side, you express your inner identity. Giving yourself the time and space to create in some way promotes self-care, stress reduction, and relaxation. Watch some crafty videos for inspiration. Try collaging, coloring, painting, doodling, or just put pen to paper and write what you know.

143

17

Power Thoughts

It's a good idea to come up with your own list of "Power Thoughts" that are unique to you. These are the thoughts that help you work through something hard, pick yourself up when you stumble, and keep yourself motivated. You can whisper these thoughts to yourself (or even yell them out) when you need that last little boost to overcome adversity. Try some of these:

I know I can handle problems.
I am capable.
I work hard.
I am resilient.
I will always keep trying.

Think of your power thoughts as your inner coaches that help you cross that finish line, no matter what.

18

JULY

Wish Upon a Star

In your life, someone might tell you to stop wishing and dreaming, and start doing. But wishes and dreams play an important role in finding the right path for your life. Not all wishes come true, but all wishes have value. They help us understand our wants and needs in this world. Go ahead and wish upon a star tonight. Set a new dream in motion by taking the time to reflect upon it.

19

JULY

One Kind Word

One kind word shared with another person can spark ripples of kindness. Compliment a friend. Offer words of encouragement and praise. Your kindness will return to you.

20
JULY

Light Your Way

Your inner strengths can act as your guiding light in any situation. We get caught up in grades and awards because that's what schools, teams, and other activities appreciate and value; it seems like almost everything ends with an award ceremony. But your inner strengths, those skills that get you through the good and the bad, those are your true lights. These skills will help you thrive for the rest of your life.

When you tap into your inner strengths, you light your own way in the dark. Inner strengths can include:

- Empathy
- Kindness
- Compassion
- Resilience
- Flexibility
- Problem-solving skills
- Stress management
- Creativity

What are your inner strengths? Think about the skills that power your light, and spend time making them shine even brighter.

21
JULY

Optimism is a Choice

You can choose to view your life through an optimistic lens, or you can choose to view it through a negative lens. Whatever choice you make sets your course. Optimism empowers you to overcome obstacles and reach your goals, while negativity will drag you down and leave you feeling helpless. Choose carefully.

22
JULY

Learn to Fly

If you want to fly, you have to learn how to let go of the things that weigh you down. That begins with identifying your own heavy load. What weighs you down? Stress, negative self-talk, fear, uncertainty, low self-esteem?

When you identify what is weighing you down, you can begin practicing positive self-talk to let it go. Instead of thinking, *I'm so stressed about school, I'll never catch up,* you can reframe it as, *I know how to organize my time, and I will do my best in school.* Let go of the heavy load that comes with stress.

23
JULY

Imagine Your Best Day

If you were only able to have one best day ever, what would you do? If you knew nothing could go wrong today, how would you spend your time? Give yourself permission to step into your imagination and create your very best day. Then take what you can from that fantasy and make it a reality.

24
JULY

Own Your Story

"Your story is what you have, what you will always have. It is something to own."

—MICHELLE OBAMA, BECOMING

25

Good Intentions

Try not to get caught up in what you think other people are doing wrong or could be doing better. Spend your time looking for the good in those around you. The world is a far more beautiful—and comforting—place when you choose to focus your energy on finding what's good.

26

Be Brave

Standing up for your beliefs, even when you feel alone, requires bravery. Listen to others to learn where they're coming from, but be willing to stand up for what you believe is right.

27

~

Redefine Success

Success isn't limited to the awards you win. You can define your own success.

    Make your own daily success checklist to see how far you come each day. It might include the following:

> *I helped someone out today.*
> *I focused on effort—the hard work I put in, not the grade or evaluation.*
> *I practiced working toward a goal.*
> *I kept a positive attitude.*
> *I worked through something difficult.*

    When you evaluate your daily successes, you build yourself up to continue working toward your larger goals.

28

JULY

Your Future is Open

Don't let past experiences limit your opportunities for the future. One bad grade doesn't mean you can't conquer that same subject another time. There are no limits to what you can achieve if you have a positive attitude, and you're willing to try again.

29

JULY

The Time for Happiness is Now

Don't wait to take steps toward finding happiness. As a busy teen, you may spend so much time checking the boxes to secure your future that you might lose out on the gift of today. Instead, choose happiness. Find little things that make you laugh or smile and make time for them each day. Chances are you have a calendar packed with things to do. Add "Be happy" to your daily to-do list to make sure that you carve out time for feeling good.

30
JULY

Replace Excuses with Changes

Instead of looking for reasons why your life isn't going the way you want it to, put your energy into making changes that will help you reach your goals. Excuses come from a place of negativity, but taking the time to figure out what you can change sets you on a positive path.

31
JULY

You Are Unique

"Don't forget—no one else sees the world the way you do, so no one else can tell the stories that you have to tell."

—CHARLES DE LINT, THE BLUE GIRL

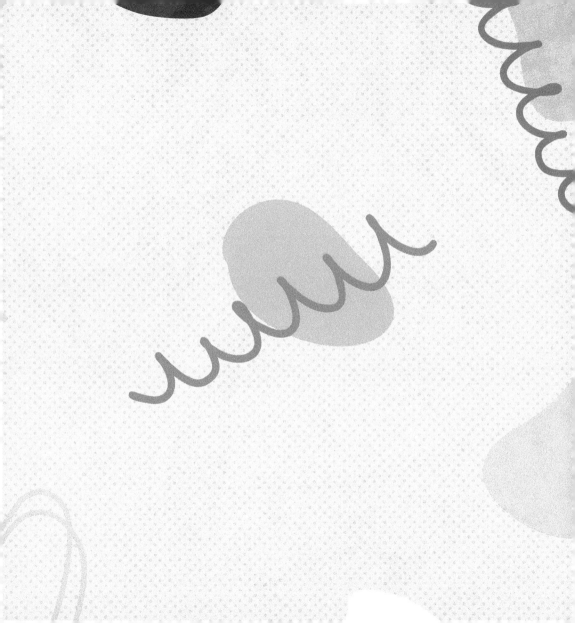

AUGUST

1

Shine Brightly

Be true to yourself and shine brightly! Begin each day with a few moments of mindful focus on who you are and what you hope to achieve. Be yourself in everything you do, and your light will shine from within.

2

Imagine Your Future Best Self

Research shows that teens who picture themselves having a happy future have greater self-esteem. To begin visualizing your happy future, try practicing one or all of these techniques:

- Close your eyes and take three deep breaths. Picture future you, doing what you love and feeling happy.
- Draw or paint your best future self.
- Journal your happy future or write it into a story.

Envisioning a happy future will improve your self-esteem today.

3
AUGUST

Trust the Process

Emotional wellness is a process for everyone at every age. It's never an overnight success. You'll have amazing days, lousy days, and everything in between, but don't give up on those in-between days. Every little bit of work you do to improve your emotional well-being makes the next day better than the last.

4
AUGUST

Beginnings are Exciting

"A blank canvas . . . has unlimited possibilities."

—STEPHANIE PERKINS, ISLA AND THE HAPPILY EVER AFTER

When you get a chance to start fresh, take advantage of it. Starting over can feel scary at first, but it's also energizing. A new start is a chance to showcase the true you.

5

AUGUST

Build a Positive Inner Circle

Your friends may not have changed over the years. If they are still filling your life with positive energy and support, that's great! But as you grow, you will change. Some of the friendships you had in elementary school or middle school may not still be there. Some friendships may remain, but to live your life to the fullest, you need a positive inner circle.

You want people in your life who lift you up and cheer you on. You also need to reciprocate that energy and be a great friend. Take some time to think about your friendships. Is it time to expand your circle? Be open to new friends and be willing to do the hard work of building friendships from the ground up.

6

AUGUST

Be a Change Maker

You can't change other people, but your actions just might be the reason someone changes. Put kindness into the world to inspire others to do the same.

Aim for Imperfection

When someone tells you that they are a "perfectionist," encourage them to be an imperfectionist instead. Aiming for perfection will only increase your stress and decrease your happiness.

No one is perfect. Everyone has something to work on, and everyone stumbles. Learn to accept the setbacks and embrace the idea of lifelong learning. Only then will you find true joy.

You Have Infinite Potential

The only limits you have to overcome are the ones you place upon yourself.

Believe in your potential.
Bet on yourself.
Say "no" to self-doubt and "yes" to possibility.

9
AUGUST

Practice Positive Talk

It's important to practice positive self-talk to yourself and to others. Take time each day to practice rephrasing your thoughts and add a positive spin. Instead of *I hate math homework*, you could reframe it as *Math isn't my favorite, but I'm looking forward to watching my favorite show when I'm done*. It's okay to vent when something is frustrating, but following it up with something positive makes the task feel less overwhelming.

10
AUGUST

Owning Up

"But there's only so long you can blame what you've been through for what you do. At some point, you gotta blame yourself."

—ANGIE THOMAS, ON THE COME UP

When you take steps to own the role you play in any situation, change can begin.

160

11

AUGUST

Mistakes are Just Mistakes

You will make mistakes. You will say the wrong thing. You will make choices you later regret. This is all part of growing up; it happens to everyone.

But your mistakes don't define you. Your mistakes are just moments. If you learn from them and apologize to those you hurt along the way, you can move forward and make positive changes. Own your mistakes, learn from them, and try again.

12

AUGUST

Kind Heart

When you have kindness in your heart, you share that positive energy with those around you. Your kind thoughts, words, and actions make a big difference in the lives of everyone you encounter.

13
AUGUST

Create Distance

You will encounter negativity sometimes. It's inevitable. Learning to distance yourself from it will help you remain positive and hopeful, even during difficult times.

> Set healthy boundaries with your friends.
> Take social media breaks when things feel negative.
> Learn to say "no" when something doesn't feel right.

14
AUGUST

Do Good

"Do good. That's all any of us can do."

—EMLYN CHAND, FARSIGHTED

If we all focus on doing good for others, the world will be a better place for everyone.

15

~

Write New Affirmations

Affirmations are positive statements that help combat negative thinking. For affirmations to work, you have to practice them daily. Try coming up with three affirmations. You want them to be powerful and easy to remember. Here are a few to get you started:

> *I will follow my dreams no matter what.*
> *If I can believe it, I can achieve it.*
> *I am complete just the way I am.*

16

~

Work Through Fear

You can't outrun your fears. You have to learn how to work through them by grounding your fears in reality. If your fear is telling you, *This is too hard. You'll never make it,* go around it by practicing self-talk and responding more positively: *I've overcome other obstacles and I can do this, too.*

17
AUGUST

Your Comfort Zone

You don't have to completely abandon your comfort zone to try something new. Your comfort zone exists for a reason. It's the place in your mind where you feel confident, safe, and secure. To reach new heights, take small steps outside of your comfort zone. Think of it like climbing a ladder: You take it one rung at a time. For instance, if you're most comfortable with one-on-one social settings, try adding one more friend to the mix to form a small group. When that feels safe and comfortable, add one more. Meaningful change is a gradual process.

18
AUGUST

Check Out

Today is a good day to check out of stress and check in to self-care.

Put down your devices.
Step into nature.
Inhale hope, exhale stress.

19

Confront Negative Filtering

Being a teen is hard. You are managing a lot of stress from a number of different sources: home, school, friendships, after-school activities, and more. When you're under stress, you might experience negative filtering, which is when you find yourself thinking something negative about almost everything. Your brain filters all of your thoughts through a negative lens.

Learn to check your negative thoughts before they affect you:

1. Write down the thoughts running through your mind.

2. Go through them one by one and take a good look at them individually.

3. Can you think of an alternative positive thought to match each negative thought?

By doing this, you work through your negative feelings and tweak your thoughts with positive words.

20
AUGUST

Listen

When you listen more than you speak, you can begin to understand people on a deeper level. People today communicate quickly and, with cell phones and other devices, often it's on screens. This can make it difficult to empathize and connect with your friends. Make space for longer conversations. Ask questions to gain understanding. Listen for the sake of listening. This is how true friendships are made.

21
AUGUST

A Mantra for Overcoming Obstacles

"I am a problem solver. I have the tools I need to work through obstacles and take the necessary steps to overcome hardship. I can do difficult things."

22

Trust Yourself

"Sometimes you're going to be faced with situations where the line isn't clear between what's right and what's wrong. Your heart will tell you to do one thing and your brain will tell you to do something different. In the end, all that's left is to look at both sides and go with your best judgment."

—CARL HIAASEN, HOOT

23

AUGUST

Use Your Time Wisely

There is never enough time in the day. But time is something that everyone craves. What matters most is not how much time you have to spend on any one thing, but how you choose to use that time. Make your time count.

24
AUGUST

Look for Opportunities

When you fall (and you will fall at some point), look for ways to get back up. When you get back up, look for new opportunities. Falling can be a chance to hit the pause button and think about your next move. Opportunities are all around you; sometimes you just need time to pay attention.

25
AUGUST

Be Kind to Your Mind

Chances are you think about what you can do to care for your physical body. But did you also know that you need to care for your mind, too? To reduce stress, worry, anxiety, and depression, you need to make healthy choices from head to toe. Try:

- Getting 8 to 10 hours of sleep each night.
- Eating a balanced diet, including more fruits and veggies.
- Exercising or moving your body every day.
- Practicing relaxation strategies.

26
AUGUST

~

Note to Self

Write yourself kind notes and hide them in different places. Put one in your backpack, one in your wallet, one under your pillow, or one in your desk. Ensure that each note is encouraging and inspiring, motivating you to keep going. Do this every few weeks so that you have notes hidden in all kinds of places. When you stumble upon one, open it up, soak in the words of kindness, and pin it to your bulletin board. Reading kind notes to yourself can boost your mood during those difficult days.

27
AUGUST

~

Make Your Own Miracles

Don't waste time waiting for a miracle to change your circumstances. Get busy creating a plan to make your own miracles. This is how you change your life.

28
AUGUST

Be a Problem Solver

There's a time and a place for venting your negative emotions. It's always a good idea to let your feelings out before they overwhelm you. It's also important to work on your problem-solving skills to face challenges as they come.

If you can see an obstacle and jump into solution-mode, you'll feel energized and empowered to conquer it. If all you can do is sit back and complain, you'll feel overwhelmed and helpless. The key to becoming a good problem solver is a subtle shift in thinking. Instead of *Oh no, what do we do now?*, meet a problem with *Let's think about how we can fix this.*

29
AUGUST

Chase the Sunset

Every sunset is a chance to put the day to rest and reset yourself. With the sunrise, you begin again.

30
AUGUST

Be Calm

When you learn to calm yourself, you learn to calm the storm around you. Get started with a few easy habits you can implement whenever you face a new challenge:

- Practice deep breathing.
- Visualize a calming memory.
- Count to 10.
- Speak with clarity and purpose.

31
AUGUST

Wait for It

Real and lasting change is difficult. In the beginning, it can be messy, and at times you might wonder if you're even headed in the right direction. Be patient with yourself. You are learning as you go, and you will see the rewards from your positive thinking as your new habits take root. It takes time.

SEPTEMBER

1
SEPTEMBER

Rise Again

Don't live in fear of low moments. There will come a time when you stumble and fall. It happens to everyone. The important thing to remember is that sometimes your lowest moments can lead to great opportunities. Take your time. Think through your options. Create a plan and rise again.

2
SEPTEMBER

Ride the Waves

"Those who don't know how to suffer are the worst off. There are times when the only correct thing we can do is to bear out troubles until a better day."

—DENG MING-DAO, EVERYDAY TAO: LIVING WITH BALANCE AND HARMONY

Helpful Notes

Never forget how great you are. When you're caught in the whirlwind of school, future planning, friendships, and busyness, it's easy to dismiss your strengths and abilities. We may not always view ourselves through the same positive lens that teachers or friends do.

1. Text a few of your family members, friends, or other people you trust to give you honest feedback. Explain that you are working on thinking more positively.

2. Ask each person to share what they think are your top three positive traits.

3. Read the responses carefully.

4. How do you feel after receiving positive feedback?

5. What can you learn from their responses?

6. Respond with gratitude and heartfelt appreciation that also includes what you admire about the other person.

4

SEPTEMBER

~

Heal

Allow yourself to heal from your past. Every experience teaches you something, even if some of the lessons feel hard and unfair. When you heal from old hurts, you open your heart to greater empathy. This will help you understand and connect with those around you and move forward with hope and compassion.

5

SEPTEMBER

~

Write

"If there's a book that you want to read, but it hasn't been written yet, then you must write it."

—TONI MORRISON

Your story matters. Put pen to paper and share it.

Words Only Have the Power You Give Them

Very few things in life are truly impossible, even when they feel that way. But your mindset determines whether or not you can overcome a difficult problem.

Declaring something *impossible* is limiting. Create possibility by saying out loud, "This may be hard, but I can find a way."

Empower Your Friends

When you see your friends struggling with something, speak up. Offer encouragement. Empower your friends to tap into positive thinking to work through their obstacles. Sharing what you've learned can light the way for someone else.

8

Take Charge

Negative thinking may arise when you feel like you have no control over your life. While you can't take charge of every little thing, you can sit down and make a list of the things that you can control. This will help you feel more positive.

Start with your day-to-day activities. Where can you make more decisions independently? Some examples might be:

- Your extracurricular activities
- Your community service goals
- Your homework schedule
- Staying on top of your grades
- How you spend your free time

Sit down with a parent or teacher and talk about what changes you want to make to increase your personal responsibility and take charge of your life.

Who Are You?

You are so many things: You are an athlete, a student, a scientist, a writer, and so much more. When people are on the outside looking in, they form judgments based on what they can see. But other people's judgments don't define you. You don't have to accept labels as truth.

Ask yourself the following questions:

Who am I?
What am I interested in?
What am I passionate about?
Who do I hope to become?

The answers to these questions hold the keys to your future.

10

Little Bits of Magic

Life throws obstacles in our way sometimes. To be human is to face the challenges we didn't see coming. It's not our job to clear away the obstacles, but it is our job to work through them, find the magic hidden beneath them, and share what we learn with the people we love. Little bits of magic are always there as long as we choose to see the good beneath the surface.

11

Daily Changes

Strive to make small daily changes toward living a positive life. Take the time to stop and smell the flowers. Give yourself permission to do the things you need to do so that you don't rush through your day. Eat foods that make you feel healthy. Walk at a pace that feels calm and comfortable. It's amazing how simple it is to change our thinking and our actions when we focus on the little things.

12
SEPTEMBER

~

Give Thanks

Be thankful for the people who helped you get to where you are. Family, teachers, coaches, friends, and many others lift you up and help you through obstacles. Write thank-you notes to acknowledge the roles those special people play in your life.

13
SEPTEMBER

~

Be Authentic

It takes courage to be authentic. It's easy to blend in with the masses, but when you step out on your own and live your life, you free your soul from the need to fit in. You were born to stand out. The world needs your unique vision. Find the courage to stand up tall and live a life of authenticity.

14
SEPTEMBER

Greatness

Greatness comes from within. Greatness is a mindset, a state of being. Once you believe you have it in you, you can share it with others and make a positive impact on the world.

15
SEPTEMBER

Be Happy for Others

Be happy for your friends when they win or find success. Chances are you don't know what obstacles they had to overcome to get there. When you lift others up by cheering them on, you show the people in your life that
you care about them and want them to find happiness, too.

16

Mind Shift

We all have negative thoughts sometimes, even when we're working toward positive thinking. When negative thoughts creep in, try this strategy to shift your thinking and feel more positive.

1. Write down your negative thought. It could be something like, *Nobody really likes me.*

2. Notice where in your body you hold your negative thoughts. Some teens are prone to getting stomachaches or headaches when they are feeling negative.

3. On a scale of 0 to 5, rate how uncomfortable or upset this thought makes you feel.

4. Write down a more positive thought. It might be, *I have two really great friends and we have fun together.*

5. On a scale of 0 to 5, rate how this positive thought makes you feel.

6. Write down three reasons the positive thought is true.

7. Read the reasons out loud and repeat the positive thought.

17
SEPTEMBER

~

A Mantra for Assertiveness

"My thoughts are important. My words are powerful.
I have the right to speak my mind."

18
SEPTEMBER

~

Quiet the Critics

Critics can sometimes be the loudest people in the room. It's easy to raise your voice when you are judging others. But success is even louder, and success can stand alone. Quiet the sound of the critics by focusing on your goals.

19

SEPTEMBER

Build Strength

You build inner strength as you learn and grow, overcoming obstacles along the way. It isn't something you're born with; it's something you cultivate by working through the hard stuff. If you feel like you don't have the strength to overcome a certain problem you face, don't give up. Reach out to a friend or family member to help you through it.

20

SEPTEMBER

Three Good Deeds

Make it a goal to do three good deeds every day. Open the door for someone, greet a stranger with a smile, help a friend with homework, or read a story to a younger sibling. Good deeds can be big or small or anything in between. It feels good to help others, and it also spreads positivity to those around you.

21

Words to Live By

You control more than you think you do, both in your life and in the lives of other people. As you go through your day consider the following:

Always be kind.
Listen to others.
Show empathy for those who are struggling.
If at first you don't succeed, figure out a new plan and try again.
If you have more, share.
Believe in yourself.
Empower others to do good things.
Leave the world better than you found it.

22
SEPTEMBER

~

Look Up

Things will get better. Even on your worst day, know that better days are ahead. When you accept yourself exactly as you are and accept your situation exactly as it is, you are ready to work through it. You might need some help. It might take some time. But things will get better. Look up often; the vast sky above is a daily reminder of how big life is. Take your time.

23
SEPTEMBER

~

Marks of Success

"Scars don't matter, little one. They are the marks of the battles we have won."

—HELEN DUNMORE, THE DEEP

24
SEPTEMBER

Just Be

Too many of us are caught up in trying to be someone we're not, or to fit into some group, but in the process, we lose ourselves. Have the courage to just be. You are enough just as you are.

25
SEPTEMBER

Make a Positivity Bucket List

A great way to practice positive thinking is to create a monthly positivity bucket list. Think about what makes you genuinely happy. Perhaps you like reading, going to the movies, hiking, or sharing a milkshake with a friend. Write down a list of 10 to 15 things that will bring you happiness. Share your list with a close friend or family member and make a pact to check off the items on this list by doing at least one item each week. In doing this, you are prioritizing positivity.

26

Daily Empowerment

Don't be so quick to jump out of bed the moment you wake up. Instead, take three deep breaths to energize your mind, stretch, and say one kind, empowering thing to yourself to get the day started. When you wake up and say something like *I'm going to work hard today and do my best,* you set yourself up for confidence and success.

27
SEPTEMBER

On Loneliness

Loneliness is common amongst teens. In a world that runs on digital and social platforms, it can be difficult to find meaningful connection. Reach out to a friend, family member, teacher, or another trusted adult for help. Sometimes the hardest words to say are the first ones, but once you get them out, you feel free from their burden. Say, "I'm lonely." Give yourself the chance to connect and find support.

Who knows? By reaching out, you might be someone else's support when they need it the most.

28

~

Join Tables

It's no big secret that the lunchroom is where you can observe the social structure of the school. Groups form, but they also close. Either you're in or you're out. If you're out, you need to keep searching. Be the change in your school by joining tables. Open your mind and your arms to new people. Break down the borders and let others in. In doing this, you create more kindness in your community and stronger bonds between friends.

There's always enough room at the table for others. Be the one creative enough to figure out how to make everyone fit.

29

~

Yes, You Can

Don't underestimate yourself. You can do more than you think. All you have to do is try. When you decide on a goal and put in a little bit of work each day, you will find confidence in your abilities.

~

Listen to the Music

Music can have a profound impact on our emotional state. Music pumps us up when we need energy, calms us down when we need to relax, and helps us work through sadness, anger, and fear. Find the songs that give you an emotional release on any given day.

List your favorite songs that fit in these categories, then make a playlist to have your anthems at the ready:

- Your happy song
- Your "cry it out" song
- Your calming song
- Your "yell through the anger" song
- Your "dance away the day" song
- Your "finally, somebody gets me" song

Let the music soothe your soul when you need a break from the day.

OCTOBER

1

Choose Positivity

Don't throw your energy toward negativity. You only have so much emotional energy to use each day. Instead, put your energy toward positive things. Choose to focus on good friendships, realistic goals, and whatever makes you happy.

2

You'll Find Your Way

It's okay if you feel stuck right now. It's okay if you're not sure which way to turn. You have hope and people in your life who care about you, and that's what matters most. You'll find your way when the time is right.

3

Be Heard

You may sometimes feel invisible. With so many adults telling you where to go and what to do, it makes sense that you sometimes feel unheard or unseen. But you can change that feeling. Assertiveness isn't just about standing up to bullies; it's also about making your mark by using your voice. Try these strategies to build your assertiveness skills:

Mirror, Mirror: Practice sharing your thoughts out loud while looking in the mirror. Stand tall, make eye contact, and smile.

Video: Make short videos on your phone. You can do this to prepare for a school presentation or simply to practice entering groups and joining conversations. Watch the video back. What did you do well? What needs work?

Role play: Ask a parent or friend to help you work through social situations that trip you up or prepare for public speaking. Have fun with it!

4

Get Cozy

There will be days when you just need to do nothing. When you're busy, it may feel strange to simply sit around. But it's important to learn to relax. Put on your cozy clothes, watch a movie, read for fun, and connect with your family. Giving yourself permission to relax helps you reset your energy levels so you can begin again and bring your best self to everything that you do.

5
OCTOBER

Prioritize

It's up to you to prioritize what's important in your life. If you make your decisions based on pressure from classmates, friends, parents, or even teachers, you aren't being true to your own needs and goals. Your life is yours to live. Your dreams belong to you. Take the time to think about what you need to do to reach your goals and set your priorities from there.

Color Outside the Lines

Remember when you were younger and it didn't matter if you colored all over the page? Remember when you weren't evaluated for every little thing, and you had the freedom to explore the world on your own terms? Close your eyes, take a deep breath, and revisit your childhood memories. Enjoy that feeling.

When you open your eyes, step back into childhood. Make a splatter painting, color fast and without care, make mud pies, or run through a sprinkler. When you give yourself permission to revisit happy feelings, you remind yourself what it's like to feel free. How can you find more simple moments of pure joy?

Find the Courage to Act

"Sometimes there's no right decision. Just the one you make at the time."

—PHAEDRA PATRICK, THE LIBRARY OF LOST AND FOUND

8

OCTOBER

Try a New Filter

In the age of social media, people love to add filters to their pictures. We can make them look bright, faded, old, or futuristic. We add text and stickers, emojis or effects. We can take what's real and alter it to make something new. But we can also do this with our thinking. When negative thinking feels powerful, try a new filter. We can add positive text and funny emojis by sending our thoughts through a positive filter.

9

OCTOBER

Embrace the Seasons

Seasons change, and so can you. Take notice of the changes in nature around you, no matter how subtle. You might notice that the leaves start to change color at the very end of the summer or that small animals, like squirrels, scurry around and bury things as fall blends into winter. Change is a gradual process in nature and in people. What small change will you make today?

10
OCTOBER

Listen to You

Your inner voice is important. It's trying to tell you all the things you need to know to find your way in this world. Listen to it. Others will always have opinions and advice on what you should do to reach your dreams, but your inner voice knows you best. Trust your gut. Follow your own lead. You can guide yourself to your own happily ever after.

11
OCTOBER

Change Your Mind

You have the right to change your mind and follow new dreams and interests. So what if you spent six years playing basketball or dedicated the last few years of your life to creative writing? If your heart isn't in it anymore and your passion fades, you're simply forcing yourself to continue out of obligation. That's no way to live a positive life. Part of life means readjusting and meeting new challenges.

You won't find your new thing until you're willing to take the chance. Go for it. Change your mind.

12

OCTOBER

~~~

Untie Your Knots

We all feel like we're tangled in knots sometimes—it's a part of being human. Worries, stress, regrets, and feelings of guilt can feel like giant knots in the pit of your stomach. You can begin to untie those knots by following these steps:

1. Take three deep breaths to release your tension.

2. Close your eyes and picture the first knot.

   What's the feeling holding that knot in place?

3. Now that you have identified the feeling, think about your triggers.

   Where did it come from?
   Why might this feeling be stuck in your gut?

4. Choose a different ending.

   What can you do to loosen this knot?
   Do you need to make an apology?
   Do you need to try something again?
   Do you need support from your parents or time to decompress?
   What might help you loosen this knot and pull it free?

13
OCTOBER

~~~

Focus on What You Have

"Be thankful for what you have; you'll end up having
more. If you concentrate on what you don't have,
you will never, ever have enough."

—OPRAH WINFREY

14
OCTOBER

~~~

Three Questions

Learning to live your life through the lens of positive thinking takes time. You might not always know what the right choice is in the moment. Asking yourself the following questions can help:

Does this help me reach my goals?
Am I experiencing positive emotions?
Is this something I feel passionate about?

15
OCTOBER

Take One Step

Your dreams will remain just dreams if all you do is think about them.
You have to take action to make your dreams come true. Sometimes
it may feel overwhelming, and that's okay. All you have to do today is
take one step toward reaching your dream. Tomorrow, you can take a
different step.

Let's say your dream is to get into an art school after high school.
Step one would be to begin researching the schools and their
requirements. What would your next steps be? Taking one small step at
a time can set your dreams in motion.

16
OCTOBER

Project Positivity

When you share your joy with others and say yes to new friends,
experiences, and ideas, you project positivity to those around you. You
become the person others look to for hope and positive energy. You
become an inspiration for others.

The World Needs You

You might find yourself wondering about your purpose or calling sometimes. It's a common thought for most people.

Here's the big secret that adults forget to tell teens: You can have more than one purpose and more than one calling. You aren't locked into one thing because you have a gift for it, and there's no rule that you have to follow a straight path from point A to point B. In fact, it's the twists and turns that help you figure out who you really are.

Take those twists and turns. See what you're made of. You'll find your way.

A Mantra for Taking Care

"The kindness, empathy, compassion, and joy that I give freely to others returns to me. I take care of my friends, and they take care of me."

19

~

Self-care Kit

It can be hard to find the time to slow down and just be. Make yourself a little self-care kit to keep in your room. Fill it with things that bring you comfort and calm. A few things to get you started:

- A chamomile tea bag
- A journal
- A stress ball
- A soft eye mask
- A favorite book

20

~

Brag a Little

In life, we are told to downplay our successes, not to brag too much. If you experience success, shout it out! You worked hard. You deserve some recognition. When your friends share their successes, cheer them on. This is how you can lift one another up and spread positive vibes.

21
OCTOBER

Feel the Love

Let your family and friends love you. Teens are often told to be independent, especially with school and meeting personal goals. This message is usually intended to inspire responsibility. But humans are not meant to go it alone. When someone loves you and cares about you, breathe it in. Soak it up. Feel grateful knowing that others are there to help you up when you fall.

22
OCTOBER

Look on the Bright Side

"I say looking on the bright side of life never killed anybody."

**—JENNY HAN, TO ALL THE BOYS
I'VE LOVED BEFORE**

Even on difficult days, you can find one good thing to focus on. Close your eyes and take a deep breath to clear your mind, and focus on the positive.

23
OCTOBER

Break Up with Stress

Letting go of stress is a choice. You don't have to walk through this world feeling stressed out and run down. It's time to break up with it.

1. Write down all of things that completely stress you out.

2. Go through your list, one stressor at a time.

   Why are you holding on to this stressor?
   Where does it come from?
   What can you replace it with?

3. Do this with each of the stressors until you cross the last one off your list.

For example: If studying for a test is taking over your life, don't let it. Don't stare at the distant future and freak out. Take small steps to ensure your journey is manageable. Soon, you'll be able to end your relationship with stress!

24

~

Be a Peacemaker

Arguments and resentment rarely result in positive change. Sure, people experience conflict. But many of us never figure out how to work *through* conflict, and some friendships may end over little things. Be the peacemaker in your group and be a good listener. Everyone wants to feel heard and understood. The next time you see your friends arguing over something, be the listener.

25

~

A Mantra for Being Gentle

Be gentle with yourself. When you are hard on yourself, the world feels unforgiving. When you are gentle, the world feels full of possibilities. If you are feeling down, empathize with yourself. Say something like:

"This is hard right now. It's okay that I don't have it all figured out. It's okay to ask for help and support when things are difficult."

26
OCTOBER

Reflect Your Light

All teens have ups and downs, good days and bad. It's completely normal to have moments where you feel like you can't find the light. On those days, lean into your support systems. Get the comfort you need. On the other days, when you feel the light practically bursting right out of you, reflect your light. Don't be afraid to show it. Share it with others. Enjoy every moment of it. The light days give us hope for the future. Soak them in.

27
OCTOBER

Get Unstuck

Negative thinking can be sticky. You might find yourself in a pattern that you don't know how to break. You can get unstuck by using self-talk. Next time you find yourself in a negative thought pattern, try this thought instead: *This is sticky thinking. This isn't my reality. I can change this situation.*

When you learn to get unstuck, you'll shift from negative thinker to problem solver.

28

—

Loving Thoughts

A good habit to stick to is to start your day with loving thoughts. How often do you race out of bed and hit the ground running without even taking a moment to really think? Consider trying this instead:

1. Set your alarm for five minutes earlier than you need. This gives you time to take a few energizing breaths and wrap yourself up in loving thoughts.

2. Say out loud to yourself "I deserve to have a great day today."

3. Give yourself a pat on the back to start the day.

Doing this will help you face the day with positive vibes.

29
OCTOBER

Let Go of Obligation

You don't need to live up to the expectations and labels other people create for you. Be open to change. Define yourself. Dig out your own path. The most direct route to happiness begins with simply being you.

30
OCTOBER

Keep Hoping

Ask yourself these questions at least once a day:

What do I hope for?
What are my hopes for those I love?
What is my hope for the world around me?
What will I do to keep these hopes alive?

Giving yourself the time to think hopeful thoughts is an exercise in positive thinking. When you're hoping, you're reaching for better. And who knows? Tomorrow just might be the day that one of those hopes comes true.

31
OCTOBER

~

Please You

It can be easy to fall into the trap of trying to please the people in your life, whether they are your teachers, parents, coaches, or even friends. It's common for teens to feel judged and evaluated by the people in their lives, and that feeling can affect how you interact with those around you.

You'll never find true happiness if you're always trying to please others. The only way to be happy is to make yourself happy, and this begins with pleasing you. Try taking some of these steps to live a life that feels positive to you:

- Work for the grade because it makes you feel confident.
- Put in extra practice so that you feel strong.
- Take the extra steps so that you always feel prepared.
- Try new styles and music because they're interesting to you.

NOVEMBER

1

Create a List of Gratitude

Instead of thinking about what you don't have, or what makes you feel down, take a moment to think about what you do have in your life; what are you grateful for? Writing things down helps you focus and increases your awareness. A gratitude list is a great way to create a permanent reminder of the good things you have in your life. And the best part is, you can add to it as you go.

Start with a few simple prompts:

I am grateful to have these people in my life:
I am grateful for these things:
I am grateful for these events:

When you focus on what you have, you open yourself up to letting more positives into your life. Tape your list above your desk or put it in a note on your phone. When you feel down or overwhelmed, check your list for a reminder.

2

When You Learn, You Thrive

"I am not afraid of storms, for I am learning how to sail my ship."

—LOUISA MAY ALCOTT, LITTLE WOMEN

3

Your Thoughts Drive Your Feelings

Self-defeating thoughts can leave you feeling down and overwhelmed. But self-confident thoughts can make you feel empowered and in control.

Your feelings are a result of the thoughts swirling around in your brain. While you can't control every negative thing that happens, you can control how you think about and respond to those negative things.

Examine your thoughts. Ask yourself why you're stuck in a negative mindset. Then reframe your thinking to include positive affirmations. Tell yourself that you can get through it, and you will.

Personal Bill of Rights

Part of setting healthy boundaries is taking the time to understand your own rights as a person. You do have the right to establish boundaries that keep you physically and emotionally safe. It's up to you if you like to hug all your friends or just fist-bump them, or even if too much sarcasm makes you uncomfortable.

Craft your own bill of rights to start thinking about your boundaries. It might look something like this:

> *I have the right to be treated with kindness.*
> *I have the right to be heard.*
> *I have the right to say no.*
> *I have the right to be respected.*
> *I have the right to walk away when something isn't right.*
> *I have the right to get help when I don't know how to handle*
> *   something.*
> *I have the right to stand up for others.*

Keep your bill of rights somewhere safe. When you feel like your boundaries aren't being respected, revisit your list. Read it out loud to make it stick. Then put your rights into action with confidence.

5

No Limits

The only limits you truly face are the ones you place upon yourself. Replace *I can't* with *I will* and see where life takes you.

6

Sing Away Stress

You will experience stress at times. It happens to everyone. Stress can feel overwhelming when you're not sure how to cope with it. A fun trick to create some emotional distance from stress is to sing about it. Let's say you're stressed about an upcoming test. Think about a favorite song and update it with your own lyrics about your stress. It might sound silly, but that's okay. Singing through your stressors and fears helps you work through your emotions and refocus on solving the problem.

7

~~~

Embrace Positivity

Focusing on the positive doesn't mean that you are denying your reality or avoiding anything negative. It means that you are grounding yourself in a positive framework so that you can work through the negative things you encounter.

Let's say your best friend suddenly turns on you, and you're iced out by your friend group. This scenario would make anyone feel helpless and hurt. When you practice positive thinking, however, you can view this from a different perspective. Yes, you're hurt and you feel isolated, but you can get through it by talking to an adult to work through your feelings. Remind yourself that you're a good friend, and there are other friends to make at your school.

You will always encounter hard situations in life. Embracing positive thinking builds you up to solve your own problems and find your own solutions. Instead of watching life happen and feeling that everything is unfair, you learn to make changes and take a new path.

8
NOVEMBER

Make Today Your Day

When you are young, time seems to be endless. Sometimes, this kind of thought can fuel procrastination. But time moves quickly, and postponing your dreams only delays your own happiness.

Make today the day that you finally put your dreams into action. Your happiness awaits.

9
NOVEMBER

Stand Tall

Be proud of who you are. You are unique. You have gifts to offer the world. Stand tall and show the world you are here to stay.

10

Stretch Your Heart

"Piglet noticed that even though he had a Very Small Heart, it could hold a rather large amount of Gratitude."

—A. A. MILNE, WINNIE-THE-POOH

Start and end your day with a simple gratitude practice. In the morning, name three people who support you. In the evening, list three things that improve your life.

11
NOVEMBER

Today Matters

Past experiences are part of our learning. We have great experiences that energize us, epic fails that teach us, and everything in between. Take those lessons and get out there and live your life to the fullest. Make today count by shining your light everywhere you go.

12
NOVEMBER

~~~

Show Appreciation

People enjoy being acknowledged and appreciated. When was the last time you slowed down enough to thank a person who plays a big role in your life? Sure, you've probably uttered "thank you" along the way, but sitting with someone and really talking about how appreciative you are of their encouragement and support is different. It sends a clear message: You are important to me.

13
NOVEMBER

~~~

Fix Your Thinking

People are always trying to figure out the best way to solve problems, but they often forget that the most important step is to fix your thinking first. You need to believe in your ability to solve your own problems. When you encounter something difficult, a positive attitude makes it easier to tackle. Try this thought instead: *I know I can handle this. I will handle this.*

14

~

Achieve

You can reach your goals. You just have to be patient. There are no overnight successes, no matter what you see on TV or in the movies. Achievement takes time and dedication. Follow these steps to get started on your path toward achievement:

1. Dream it.

2. Envision it.

3. Plan it.

4. Break it down.

5. Take the first step.

6. Carry on.

15

Enjoy What You Have

Don't waste a single moment of your time worrying about what you might have missed. Sure, you've probably missed something exciting at some point, but your life continues to move forward. When you focus on what you might miss, you choose to live in frustration and resentment. When you focus on what you have and what you're doing, you choose to live in happiness and appreciation.

16

Name It

*"It's a lot easier to understand things
once you name them."*

—CARRIE JONES, NEED

~

Lighten Your Emotional Load

Teens seem to have a lot on their plates. This can result in unnecessary stress, which affects relationships, school, personality, memory, and everything else. Just like you need to fill your plate with a balanced meal, you also need to balance your emotional plate.

1. Start by drawing a circle on a piece of paper.

2. Fill the circle with the many things you have to juggle (sports, friends, family, etc.) that might trigger stress when your plate is overloaded.

3. Take time to consider every little stressor in your life. What do you need to create balance?

4. Take a red pen and cross out the sources of stress that you can remove.

5. Take a blue pen and circle sources of stress that you can manage with better coping skills.

6. Keep rearranging your plate until it feels healthy and manageable.

7. Now change your life, with your new plate in mind, starting today.

18

~

Don't Let Fear Hold You Back

Fear is a powerful emotion. It can consume you and make it feel like your dreams are out of reach. But fear can also overreact. Don't let your fears about a certain outcome hold you back from achieving your dreams. Try this grounding technique when your fear is taking over:

> *This is just fear talking. I am feeling afraid of . . .*
> *The reason I am afraid of this is because . . .*
> *This fear might not be true because . . .*
> *A more accurate statement would be . . .*
> *I can overcome this fear by . . .*

Labeling your fears for what they are and working through them helps you get to the other side. When you do that, you can begin to move forward.

19

~

Reset

Sit in a comfortable position with your feet on the ground. Place one hand on your heart and one hand on your stomach so you can feel the rise and fall of your breath.

Notice your body:
- Relax the muscles in your face, neck, and shoulders.
- Release the tension in your arms and legs.

Notice your breath:
- Inhale through your nose, exhale through your mouth.
- Feel your stomach rise, hold, and fall with each breath.

Notice your responses:
- **Thoughts:** Is your mind wandering?
- **Physical reactions:** Are your muscles relaxing? Does your body feel calm, tense, or something else?
- **Feelings:** What are you feeling as you breathe? Are you calm, happy, mad, or sad?

This exercise will help you become more aware of how you carry your stress and what it feels like to let that stress go.

226

20

Get Organized

Clutter and disorganization can fuel stress and anxiety, especially for teens dealing with exams, projects, and busy schedules. Carve out 30 minutes each week to clean up your workspace, organize your backpack, and clear the clutter from your room. Your brain will thank you for it.

21
NOVEMBER

The Journey is the Gift

"It's not about the destination. It's getting there that's the good part."

—MORGAN MATSON, AMY & ROGER'S EPIC DETOUR

When striving for a goal, be sure to set small milestones to meet each week and take time to reflect upon them and feel good about your progress.

22
NOVEMBER

Daily Gratitude

When you end your day with gratitude, you fall asleep taking comfort in good things. Take a few moments to think through the positive things that happened today.

- Name three things you are grateful for.
- List three great things that happened today.
- Set three positive intentions, or things, you can do to improve your day, for tomorrow.

23
NOVEMBER

A Mantra for Self-Love

*"The more I like myself, the more others will like me.
When I have confidence, I show others that
I am comfortable in my own shoes."*

24

Try Single-tasking

The human brain wasn't designed to multitask. Your brain engages in task-switching—moving back and forth between tasks, sometimes very quickly—when it's trying to do too many things at once. When you're engaged in task-switching, you're likely not doing any one thing particularly well or efficiently. It's also exhausting.

Be mindful about single-tasking. Try these tips to learn to focus on one task at a time:

- Put your mobile device on airplane mode when you're working to stop the notifications from grabbing your attention.
- Put pen to paper to create a schedule that keeps you on track. Add breaks for snacks and movement.
- Create a calming work environment. Find a clean area with minimal clutter and distractions.
- Focus on reasonable expectations. You will experience fatigue, and your mind will begin to wander if you don't take breaks.

25
NOVEMBER

Encourage

Discouraging people are dream-dashers. They declare the problem impossible before they even attempt to solve it. Encouragers are dream-lifters. They look for solutions and amplify a positive message of hope. Be an encourager. Make a difference.

26
NOVEMBER

Recycle and Reset

You can . . .

> Reset
> Readjust
> Restart
> Refocus
> As many times as you need to.

There are no limits on trying again.

27

Self-kindness Script

With the constant pressure to measure up, life can feel like an endless roller coaster of stress sometimes. Write your own self-kindness scripts that you can use when you're feeling critical about yourself. You can use the examples below, or you can rewrite them to make them work for you.

May my day be filled with kindness.
May I be calm, happy, and healthy.
May I feel safe, secure, and free from worry.
May I feel love and affection from my family.
May I be gentle with my thoughts today.

28

NOVEMBER

Give Thanks

It's always a good idea to be thankful for the friends who brighten your life. Message each of your close friends today. Let them know how thankful you are to have them in your life.

29

Be Self-confident

When you believe in yourself, you never have to worry about proving your worth to others. Self-confidence is knowing that you are happy just the way you are and that you are worth knowing, no matter what other people say.

30

~

Mindfully Upset

Bad moments will happen. You will feel overwhelmed sometimes. But ignoring big feelings won't actually help resolve them. Mindfulness is a very useful tool when you feel overwhelmed and upset. Try this:

Label: Recognize what emotions you are experiencing, label them, and own them.

Sit with it: Accept the situation as it is. Acknowledge what you're feeling and what triggered it.

Evaluate with kindness: Notice your thoughts and the physical responses associated with your emotions. Be gentle with yourself. This is not a time to criticize yourself; this is a time to figure out how you got here.

Think it out: Consider what would help you feel better in this moment. Do you need support from an adult? Would a walk around the block help you clear your mind? Find a solution to work through the emotion so that you feel calm again.

DECEMBER

1

Who Are You?

Instead of obsessing about who you think you should be, try examining who you already are. You may find that you are just right, exactly the way you are.

1. Make a list of the different roles you play in your life.

   Who are you to different people (e.g., daughter, son, friend, teammate, student, grandchild, etc.)?

2. List as many as you can think of.

3. Now, make a separate list of your positive attributes.

   What makes you a great friend?
   What are your strengths?
   How do you show others you care?

4. Take time to look at both lists and really appreciate everything you wrote down.

   Tuck these lists away somewhere safe and revisit them every month. What can you add?

2

~~~

Accept Conflict

You may not always be able to avoid conflict, but you can learn how to accept and cope with it. To communicate during a conflict, it can be helpful to use "I feel" statements. This reduces blame and keeps the focus on how you're feeling about the event. An example might be, "I feel embarrassed when you post candid pictures of me. Please ask me first." You're not blaming or making accusations, but you are asserting your feelings and needs with confidence.

When you accept that conflict is a natural part of life, you learn how to navigate it more easily.

3
DECEMBER

~~~

Go with the Flow

"If you just go with the flow, no matter what weird things happen along the way, you always end up exactly where you belong."

—TOM UPTON, *JUST PLAIN WEIRD*

4
DECEMBER

Believe

Never stop believing in the things that give you hope.

> Believe in kindness.
> Believe in friendship.
> Believe in love.
> Believe in happiness.
> Believe in positivity.

Belief is what sustains you when need to get through the hard days. Above all, believe in yourself.

5
DECEMBER

Light Up the Room

When you enter a room, stand tall, make eye contact, and smile. This shows people that you are happy to be and boosts your self-confidence. Go ahead! Put your best foot forward and shine.

A Work in Progress

Changing your mindset requires work and dedication. You have to practice self-discipline. It's easy to walk away when things are hard and say it didn't work, or it's not making a difference. By practicing positive thinking during the most difficult times, you teach yourself to keep trying. The more you try, the easier it becomes. When that pesky negative voice speaks up, respond with: I can do this. *Changing my mindset is a work in progress.*

Choose Happy

Every morning, you have two choices: happiness or unhappiness. It's up to you. If you choose happiness, think about what that means. Surround yourself with positive people, do things that inspire you, and make decisions that elevate your goals and fit your positive mindset.

8
DECEMBER
~

Create Your Vision

When you can envision success, you are more likely to reach your goals. Anticipate that you might hit some bumps along the way, but your vision of success can include plans to overcome obstacles.

1. Get a poster board, or create a digital one, and write your goal in giant letters across the top.

2. Take a deep breath and smile. Doesn't it feel good to write it down?

3. List your benchmarks (your smaller steps) underneath.

4. On one side, map out anticipated obstacles.

5. On the other side, write down the supports you need to reach this goal.

6. Fill in the blank spaces with words of encouragement and favorite inspirational quotes.

7. Take a step back and review your vision of success.

Tomorrow, put your plan into action by working toward that first benchmark.

9

Good Vibes Crew

Surround yourself with people who celebrate you. To be blanketed by people who simply tolerate you is to hold yourself back from happiness. Find the people whose eyes sparkle when you enter the room and stick with them.

10

Go for It

Sometimes you need to do something you don't normally do to give yourself a break.

> Eat the chocolate chips before baking the cookies.
> Splash barefoot in the puddles during the storm.
> Chase the butterflies through the park.
> Scribble on the page without thinking about what you're making.

Go for it. Give your mind a rest today by stepping outside of yourself and setting your spirit free.

11

Radiate Empathy

Expressing empathy toward others amplifies their positive energy. Teens hear a lot about the benefits of empathy at school and at home, but they aren't always given specific guidance on how to practice it. To start practicing empathy:

Use active listening skills. Do not listen to respond; listen to listen. Ask questions if you don't understand something; otherwise, make eye contact, nod, and listen.

Convey understanding. The best thing you can say to a friend is, "That sounds hard. I'm really sorry. How can I help?"

Respect boundaries. Your friend might not want help. They might simply want to vent. Respect that.

Don't share conversations. Part of showing empathy toward others is holding their stories close. Don't gossip or share information without permission.

Put yourself in your friend's shoes. Try to think about how it might feel to go through what your friend is going through. Be kind. Check in often.

Don't judge. Don't criticize or share opinions. Just be supportive.

12
DECEMBER

Stress is Temporary

Stress isn't permanent. You can work through your stress, and you will solve your problems. When you feel overwhelmed, try saying to yourself: *This is temporary. I will feel happy again.*

13
DECEMBER

Trust Your Inner Compass

It's natural to look to adults for help and validation when you're feeling uncertain, but if you seek outside assistance each time you face a problem, you'll never learn to trust yourself. Your instincts are trustworthy when you take the time to nurture them, and your inner compass is there to point you in the right direction. When you feel uncertain, close your eyes and ask yourself these questions:

> *What is my gut reaction?*
> *What are my instincts trying to tell me?*
> *Where does my compass point?*

Live Your Best Life

Every day is an opportunity to live your best life. Consider some of the following, while living your day:

- Read for fun.
- Keep good company.
- Smile often.
- Learn from others.
- Find a creative outlet.
- Be yourself.
- Love your people.
- Dream.

And then repeat.

15

~~~

Write a Happy Story

Write a story of happiness today. It can be fiction or nonfiction, long or short. Tell a story about someone overcoming obstacles to find true happiness.

> What hoops does your character have to jump through?
> How do they get over those hurdles?
> What does pure happiness mean to your character?

Writing a story of happiness frames your thoughts in a positive perspective. Your life might not mirror that of your main character, but you might learn something from the story.

16
DECEMBER

~~~

Footprints

We all leave footprints everywhere we go: at school, the places we visit, and on the hearts of the people who care about us. Be mindful of the footprints you leave behind.

17

DECEMBER

~

Find Inspiration

Inspiration won't find you; you have to get out in the world and look for it. Walk through nature. Listen to the sounds around you. Read for fun. Find the characters that speak to you. Listen to music as much as possible. Think about what moves you.

No two people are the same, but everyone needs to find their own sources of inspiration. What is yours?

18

DECEMBER

~

Cheer on Your Friends

Empower your friends to shine in their own way and to reach for their dreams. Offer to help them realize their goals. Cheer when they hit their benchmarks. Celebrate together. Practicing a positive mindset can be done alone, but it feels even better when done with friends and family. Elevate your positivity by bringing your friends and loved ones into the fold.

19
DECEMBER

Lead the Way

Teens face a lot of peer pressure these days, and it might feel like following the crowd is the easiest thing to do.

Never follow without knowing where you're heading.
Never fall in line without asking the hard questions first.

Be a leader. Build your own path of positive thinking and choices and invite others to join you along your journey.

20
DECEMBER

Make it Count

Life isn't a rehearsal for opening night of the show. Life is opening night. Sure, you'll make mistakes and have second (and third) chances, but when you make decisions, make them with intention. Make your mark on this world by figuring out who you are, who you want to be, and what you can do to make the world a more positive place. Whatever you do, make it count.

21
DECEMBER

~

Enjoy Alone Time

So many teens fear being alone in this modern and busy world. They don't know what to do, and they don't want to miss out on something fun. You know what's really fun? Alone time. When you have the freedom to be alone and enjoy the quiet, you find the time to develop new dreams and just be. You find the space to love yourself completely.

22
DECEMBER

~

Know Your Limits

Everyone has a limit. When you feel yourself becoming overloaded with stress, slow down. Listen to what your mind and body are trying to tell you. Pushing yourself past your emotional limit won't help you reach your dreams any faster. In fact, it might slow you down with exhaustion. Take a mental health day, binge watch your favorite show, or eat comfort foods. Your dreams will still be there tomorrow.

23
DECEMBER

Dream Big

*"Everyone must dream. We dream to give ourselves hope. To stop dreaming—
well, that's like saying you can never change your fate. Isn't that true?"*

—AMY TAN, *THE HUNDRED SECRET SENSES*

24
DECEMBER

Keep Your Door Open

One thing that can happen when you have very specific goals is that
you become laser-focused on them to a point where other options may
be overlooked. Always keep the door open for opportunities. You never
know when something will inspire you and send you in a new direction.

25
DECEMBER

Use the Stoplight

When you feel worried or anxious about something, try the stoplight technique to cope with your feelings.

Red: Identify the source of the worry, stress, or anxiety.

Yellow: Think about options to get through the feeling. Examples might include deep breathing, a 10-minute yoga sequence on an app, a mindfulness session, or talking to a friend.

Green: Choose the best strategy and act.

You might feel "stuck" when anxious thoughts take over, but visualizing a stoplight while working through the thought will help you overcome your anxious thoughts and get back to doing what makes you happy.

250

26

~

Give Your Best

All you can do on any given day is your best. To your friends, your family, your schoolwork, your activities and goals, all you can give is your best. Some days that will be enough; other days you'll come up short. That's okay. Every day is a new day to give your best.

27

~

Get Started

Sometimes getting started is the hardest part of working toward a goal or changing a mindset. Getting started can feel overwhelming. What you can do is break it down until you find a very small, manageable starting point. Instead of thinking, *I'll use positive thinking all day, every day, starting today,* it's better to begin with something small and tangible like, *I will start each day by listing three things I'm looking forward to.* Practice that for a couple of weeks, then add something new.

28
DECEMBER

Love Your Imperfections

Your perceived imperfections are what make you human. Love them. Make peace with them. Know that you are the only you around, and that's something to love.

29
DECEMBER

Look for the Light

A bad moment during the day can sometimes feel like it ruins everything. One unkind comment or one low grade could send you into a tailspin of feeling awful. You can't control every little thing that happens during the day, but you can choose to look for the light instead of allowing one negative experience to ruin your whole day.

Try saying to yourself: *That happened, and that feels awful, but something good that happened was . . .*

30

A Mantra for Belonging

"I am right where I am supposed to be, learning what I am meant to learn. I belong here."

31

Three Positive Thoughts

End this year with three positive thoughts about yourself.

1. What progress did you make this year?
2. What did you learn?
3. What is one thing that happened that changed your life for the better?

Take these thoughts into the New Year as you work toward toward positive thinking.

FURTHER EXPLORATION

Books

The Self-Love Workbook for Teens: A Transformative Guide to Boost Self-Esteem, Build a Healthy Mindset, and Embrace Your True Self by Shainna Ali, PhD

Discover how to change your attitude, build your self-confidence, and discover who you really are using this guided journal.

The Mindfulness Journal for Teens: Prompts and Practices to Help You Stay Cool, Calm, and Present by Jennie Marie Battistin, LMFT

This interactive guide will help you slow down and learn to work through your stressors using simple prompts and exercises that you can use each day.

Letting Go of Anger Card Deck: 54 Cards to Help Teens Tame Frustration by Dr. Jeffrey Bernstein

Use this deck of cards to learn to identify and understand your anger, and to learn calming techniques to combat anger.

The 7 Habits of Highly Effective Teens by Sean Covey

This roadmap to working through the teen years will help you improve self-esteem, build friendships, and set and reach your goals.

The Depression Workbook for Teens: Tools to Improve Your Mood, Build Self-Esteem, and Stay Motivated by Katie Hurley, LCSW

This book is filled with helpful exercises specifically designed for teens to help you work through negative thinking and find joy.

The Essential Self-Compassion Workbook for Teens: Overcome Your Inner Critic and Fully Embrace Yourself by Katie Krimer, LCSW

This interactive guide is packed with strategies to help you calm your inner critic and learn to love yourself.

The Ultimate Self-Esteem Workbook for Teens: Overcome Insecurity, Defeat Your Inner Critic, and Live Confidently by Megan MacCutcheon, LPC

This workbook offers tools to help you boost your self-esteem and practice replacing negative self-talk with positive self-talk.

The 5-Minute Happiness Journal: Practices to Help You Tap Into Joy Every Day by Leslie Marchand

This book is packed with 100 prompts to help you increase your gratitude and happiness in just a few minutes a day.

Stuff That Sucks: A Teen's Guide to Accepting What You Can't Change and Committing to What You Can by Ben Sedley, PhD

Read this compassionate guide to learn how to accept and work through the hard stuff and transform your thinking.

Ignite Your Spark: Discovering Who You Are from the Inside Out by Patricia Wooster

This interactive guide shows you how to forge your own path, engage your passions, and become the person you want to be.

Apps

Calm

This meditation app will help you sleep better, boost your confidence, and keep you feeling calm and grounded.

Grateful

This gratitude journal gives you specific prompts to help you slow down and record your feelings of gratitude.

Happify

This app uses games and activities to decrease stress and anxiety, and help you tap into positive thinking.

Unique Daily Affirmations

Record your own voice reading daily positive affirmations to give yourself the boost of positivity you need throughout the day.

Websites

TeenLineOnline.org

Find support from teen counselors during difficult times.

TeenMentalHealth.org

Get information about mental health, resources, and support.

REFERENCES

Abrams, Abiola. *The Sacred Bombshell Handbook of Self-Love: The 11 Secrets to Feminine Power*. Love University Press, 2014.

Alcott, Louisa May. *Little Women*. New York: Signet Classics, 2004.

Alexander, Kwame. *Rebound*. Boston: HMH Books for Young Readers, 2018.

Barrie, J. M. *The Little White Bird*. Cookhill, Worcestershire: Pook Press, 2013.

Bingham, John. *No Need for Speed: A Beginner's Guide to the Joy of Running*. New York: Rodale Books, 2002.

BrainyQuote. "Tina Fey Quotes." Accessed June 22, 2020. Brainyquote.com /quotes/tina_fey_564256.

Brees, Drew and Chris Fabry. *Coming Back Stronger: Unleashing the Hidden Power of Adversity*. Carol Stream, IL: Tyndale House Publishers, 2010.

Chand, Emlyn. *Farsighted*. New York: Blue Crown Press, 2011.

Coelho, Paulo. *The Alchemist*. San Francisco: HarperOne, 2014.

Dahl, Roald. *The Twits*. London: Puffin Books, 2004.

De Lint, Charles. *The Blue Girl*. New York: Firebird Books, 2006.

Dessen, Sarah. *Along for the Ride*. New York: Viking Books for Young Readers, 2009.

DiCamillo, Kate. *Flora & Ulysses: The Illuminated Adventures*. Somerville, MA: Candlewick Press, 2013.

Donoghue, Emma. *Room*. New York: Little Brown & Company, 2010.

Dunmore, Helen. *The Deep*. New York: HarperCollins Publishers, 2007.

Eagleson, Claire, Sarra Hayes, Andrew Mathews, Gemma Perman, and Colette R. Hirsch. "The Power of Positive Thinking: Pathological Worry is Reduced by Thought Replacement in Generalized Anxiety Disorder." *Behaviour Research and Therapy*

78 (March 2016): 13–18.

Faulkner, William. *The Mansion*. New York: Vintage Books, 2011.

Fredrickson, Barbara. *Positivity: Groundbreaking Research Reveals How to Embrace the Hidden Strength of Positive Emotions, Overcome Negativity, and Thrive*. New York: Crown, 2009.

Fredrickson, Barbara L., Michael A. Cohn, Kimberly A. Coffey, Jolynn J. Pek, and Sandra M. Finkel. "Open Hearts Build Lives: Positive Emotions, Induced through Loving-Kindness Meditation, Build Consequential Personal Resources." Journal of Personality and Social Psychology 95, no. 5 (November 2008): 1045–1062. doi.org/10.1037/a0013262.

Goodreads. "Barack Obama > Quotes." Accessed May 29, 2020. Goodreads.com/author/quotes/6356.Barack_Obama.

Goodreads. "Gloria Steinem > Quotes." Accessed May 29, 2020. Goodreads.com/author/quotes/57108.Gloria_Steinem.

Goodreads. "Inspiring Quotes > Stephen Hawking." Accessed May 29, 2020. Goodreads.com/quotes/tag/inspiring-quotes.

Goodreads. "Lucille Ball > Quotes." Accessed May 29, 2020. Goodreads.com/author/quotes/86608.Lucille_Ball.

Goodreads. "Mark Twain > Quotes." Accessed May 29, 2020. Goodreads.com/author/quotes/1244.Mark_Twain?page=2.

Goodreads. "Maya Angelou > Quotes." Accessed May 29, 2020. Goodreads.com/author/quotes/3503.Maya_Angelou.

Goodreads. "Mother Teresa > Quotes." Mother Teresa. Accessed May 29, 2020. Goodreads.com/author/quotes/838305.Mother_Teresa?page=2.

Goodreads. "Oprah Winfrey > Quotes." Accessed May 29, 2020. Goodreads.com/author/quotes/3518.Oprah_Winfrey.

Goodreads. "Toni Morrison > Quotes." Accessed June 22, 2020. Goodreads.com/author/quotes/3534.Toni_Morrison.

Goodreads. "Sports Inspirational Quotes." Accessed August 14, 2020. https://www

.goodreads.com/quotes/tag/sports-inspirational.

Green, John. *Looking for Alaska*. New York: Speak, 2006.

Han, Jenny. *To All the Boys I've Loved Before*. New York: Simon & Schuster Books for Young Readers, 2014.

Hiaasen, Carl. *Hoot*. New York: Yearling Books, 2006.

Itejere, Larry. *The Silver Arrow*. Los Gatos, CA: Smashwords Editions, 2011.

Jones, Carrie. *Need*. London: Bloomsbury Publishing, 2008.

Kline, Christina Baker. *A Piece of the World*. New York: William Morrow, 2017.

Lauritsen, Aaron. *100 Days Drive: The Great North American Road Trip*. Self-published, CreateSpace, 2016.

Lee, Harper. *To Kill a Mockingbird*. New York: Harper Perennial Modern Classics, 2006.

Lowry, Lois. *The Giver*. Boston: Houghton Mifflin, 1993.

Lupica, Mike. *Miracle on 49th Street*. New York: Philomel Books, 2006.

Martin, George R. R. *A Game of Thrones: A Song of Fire and Ice*. New York: Bantam Books, 2006.

Matson, Morgan. *Amy & Roger's Epic Detour*. New York: Simon & Schuster Books for Young Readers, 2010.

Merriam Webster Online. "Empathy." Accessed May 29, 2020, Merriam-webster.com/dictionary/empathy.

Meyer, Stephenie. *Twilight*. New York: Little, Brown & Co, 2005.

Milne, A. A. *Winnie-the-Pooh*. New York: Dutton Juvenile, 2001.

Ming-Dao, Deng. *Everyday Tao: Living with Balance and Harmony*. San Francisco: HarperOne, 1996.

Obama, Michelle. *Becoming*. New York: Crown Publishing Group, 2018.

Oliver, Lauren. *Delirium*. New York: HarperTeen, 2011.

Owens, Rhea L., and Meagan M. Patterson. "Positive Psychological Interventions for Children: A Comparison of Gratitude and Best Possible Selves Approaches." Journal of Genetic Psychology 174, no. 4 (July/August 2013): 403-28. doi.org/10.1080/00221325.2012.697496.

Palacio, R. J. *Wonder*. New York: Alfred A. Knopf, 2012.

Patrick, Phaedra. *The Library of Lost and Found*. New York: Park Row Books, 2019.

Perkins, Stephanie. *Isla and the Happily Ever After*. New York: Dutton, 2014.

Picoult, Jodi. *Change of Heart*. New York: Atria Books, 2008.

Redwine, C. J. *Defiance*. New York: Balzer + Bray, 2012.

Reynolds, Jason. *Ghost*. New York: Atheneum/Caitlyn Dlouhy Books, 2016.

Sloan, Holly Goldberg. *Counting By 7s*. New York: Dial Books for Young Readers, 2013.

Tan, Amy. *The Hundred Secret Senses*. New York: Ivy Books, 1996.

Telgemeier, Raina. *Smile*. New York: Scholastic/Graphix, 2010.

Thomas, Angie. *On the Come Up*. Thorndike Press Large Print, 2019.

Upton, Tom. *Just Plain Weird*. Self-published, CreateSpace, 2008.

White, E. B. *Charlotte's Web*. New York: HarperCollins Publishers, 2001.

Woodson, Jacqueline. *Brown Girl Dreaming*. New York: Nancy Paulsen Books, 2014.

ACKNOWLEDGMENTS

Thank you to the many teens who have rolled through my office over the years, teaching me as much as I teach them. This one's for you.

As always, heaping piles of gratitude for my husband, Sean, who lifts me up and cheers me on. And to Riley and Liam, for sharing me with the world once again in my ongoing attempt to promote the power of optimism, empathy, and finding happiness. You are my everything, and you always will be. Keep writing. The world needs your voices, too.

ABOUT THE AUTHOR

KATIE HURLEY, LCSW, is a child and adolescent psychotherapist, parenting educator, public speaker, and writer. Hurley is the author of *No More Mean Girls: The Secret to Raising Strong, Confident, and Compassionate Girls; The Depression Workbook for Teens: Tools to Improve Your Mood, Build Self-Esteem, and Stay Motivated;* and *The Happy Kid Handbook: How to Raise Joyful Children in a Stressful World.* Hurley covers mental health, child and adolescent development, and parenting for a number of publications. She earned her BA in psychology and women's studies from Boston College and her MSW from the University of Pennsylvania.

CPSIA information can be obtained
at www.ICGtesting.com
Printed in the USA
LVHW011459101221
705757LV00004B/4

9 781647 396404